MW01630082

Bruno Sacco

LEADING MERCEDES-BENZ DESIGN
1975–1999

Bruno Sacco

LEADING MERCEDES-BENZ DESIGN
1975–1999

NIK GREENE

THE CROWOOD PRESS

First published in 2020 by
The Crowood Press Ltd
Ramsbury, Marlborough
Wiltshire SN8 2HR

enquiries@crowood.com

www.crowood.com

This impression 2024

British Library Cataloguing-in-Publication Data
A catalogue record for this book is available from the British Library.

ISBN 978 1 78500 717 0

Designed and typeset by Guy Croton Publishing Services,
West Malling Kent

Printed and bound in India by Parksons Graphics Pvt. Ltd.

CONTENTS

PREFACE & ACKNOWLEDGEMENTS

In general, I don't have heroes in my life. Having encountered many 'celebrities' over the years, I tend not to be fazed or awed by their presence. However, once in a while, I have had the privilege of meeting someone who came as close to what I would probably class as a hero, should I take the time to define the term. Bruno Sacco, someone whose work I had followed since my early teens, is one such person.

In the days before the internet, when information was not so easily acquired, I used to travel regularly to main dealerships to ask for car brochures and catalogues. I would collect car magazines and books and stand at a library terminal scanning newspaper articles, looking for a whisper of what the next model of Mercedes-Benz would look like. Occasionally, there would be a reference to a stylist or designer by the name of Bruno Sacco. Never in my wildest dreams did I think that I would, one day, be standing in front of this man.

Writing this book has been exciting, but it has also been frustrating. I have met and spoken with many people connected with either Bruno Sacco or design at Mercedes-Benz and not one person spoke of him or his work with anything other than praise and admiration. During the hours I spent with him, he was endlessly humble and modest about his achievements. There was not a hint of ego.

At the end of our first meeting, I asked him whether he had ever thought of writing an autobiography, or agreeing to someone telling his story. He looked at me in dismay. 'Why?' he said.' I did nothing on my own. Everything we did, we did as a team; everything we did, we did for Mercedes-Benz. If you want to write about me, write about design.'

So here it is. The only way I could honour one of the greatest designers in automotive history was to write his story through the history of design, honouring the people he honoured, and showing his talent through his work and not through his ego.

ACKNOWLEDGEMENTS

At times, writing can be a solitary act and it can feel especially lonely as one stares at a screen with dry eyes for hours on end. However, there are times when putting a book together is anything but solitary, especially when it is a book such as this.

I hope the reader will take the time to read through these acknowledgments and not just pass them by in search of the main content, because that content just wouldn't be there if it wasn't for a significant number of people. I cannot list them all here, as there are too many of them, but you know who you are, and I thank sincerely every one of you.

I must start with Trudy, my long-suffering wife who not only has had to put up the silence behind my concentration, but also the breaks in the silence as I eagerly expect her to be as excited as I am about a new snippet of information…. Knowing you are in my eyeline when I turn my chair means everything. I thank you for that as much as I thank you for your patience and understanding.

Even though I have been requested not to name individuals, I have to thank Daimler AG for their support and information, which has been so freely given by everyone I met. My time at Untertürkheim and Sindelfingen has been invaluable.

My sincere thanks to everyone at the Daimler archives for your hard work, patience, support and permissions. If it wasn't for you all, this just would not have been possible.

To Harald Leschke, to Stephen Ferrada, to Harry Neimann, to Paul Bracq, a special thank you to you all for donating your precious time and insight, for answering my rambling emails, and for allowing me to use your personal images.

Herr Sacco, I am honoured; thank you from the bottom of my heart.

Nik Greene
November 2019

MILESTONES OF MERCEDES-BENZ DESIGN

1886

Carl Benz presents the world's first car in the form of his patented 'motor vehicle for operation by gas engine'. The structure of the three-wheeler, which is inspired by the design of a bicycle, is an expression of engineering in its purest form.

1901

The Mercedes 35 HP establishes an independent form for the automobile and is regarded as the first modern car. The honeycomb radiator, which is organically integrated into the front of the vehicle, becomes a hallmark of the brand.

1905

The Daimler-Motoren-Gesellschaft in Untertürkheim sets up its own body-manufacturing shop.

1909

The famous Blitzen-Benz record-breaker and racing car is the first vehicle on which the design is clearly influenced by aerodynamic considerations.

1910

A defining point is reached in the development of automotive design: a bulge below the windscreen, referred to as a 'cowl' or 'torpedo', links the chassis and engine box assembly with the body and passenger compartment to form an

A worker constructing a flat-plan crankshaft in the engine manufacturing building.

The first building on the new factory grounds of the Daimler Motoren Gesellschaft in Untertürkheim was the manufacturing centre. Offices were located in the front section of the building. (Photo taken around 1905.)

The 1910 automobile, with its newly harmonious form.

organic whole. With its new, smooth walls and continuous beltline, the automobile now has a harmonious form.

1911

In parallel with the flat honeycomb radiator, DMG develops a second characteristic radiator form: the pointed version is used principally for the sporty and high-power models in the range.

1920

The DMG factory in Sindelfingen starts manufacturing Mercedes bodies.

1932

Hermann Ahrens takes charge of the special vehicles department at the Mercedes-Benz Sindelfingen plant.

1934

With the elegant, flowing lines of its Hermann Ahrens-designed body, the Type 500K and its 1936 successor, the 540K, represent highlights of Mercedes-Benz design, especially in the Special Roadster version, which is regarded as the ultimate dream car of the 1930s. The coupé variant establishes the modern coupé tradition at Mercedes-Benz.

1953

The Type 180, with its integral body structure, is the model which brings the classic Mercedes-Benz design into the modern era. The wings and headlamps are fully integrated into the main body, which also encloses the engine compartment and the luggage compartment at the rear. Above this rises the passenger compartment, which has a window area that is large by the standards of the day.

1954

The legendary 300 SL is introduced, with gullwing doors, new, unconventional proportions. Also new is a flat version of the Mercedes-Benz radiator grille, which becomes a defining feature of the front design of the SL sports cars. This super sports car is the last word in automotive design in its day.

1957

The vertical headlamps with integral indicators introduced in the 300 SL Roadster become a defining stylistic device, which features in the front design of Mercedes-Benz passenger cars until the beginning of the 1970s.

Sindelfingen carpentry workshop creating body shells.

W198 300 SL roadster showing the front headlights.

With its clear, geometric lines, the Mercedes-Benz 600 set new standards for the class of exclusive and luxurious prestige vehicles.

1959

The Mercedes-Benz 220, 220 S and 220 SE six-cylinder saloons make their debut, with restrained tailfins that are officially described as 'guide bars'. The tailfin Mercedes is also the world's first vehicle with a rigid occupant compartment and energy-absorbing crumple zones — attributes which mark the beginning of a new chapter in the field of safety technology.

1961

The two-door coupé variant of the 220 SE has its own distinctive design treatment, a notable characteristic being the absence of the saloon model's tailfins. The clean lines of the timelessly beautiful coupé dominate Mercedes-Benz design in the 1960s.

1963

The 230 SL appears with surprising new proportions and lines — as well as the unmistakable 'Pagoda' roof, a removable hard top whose special form not only looks good but also offers greater rigidity and, therefore, safety.

1971

The new 350 SL sports-car model and the S-Class of 1972 give visible and tangible expression to the integrated safety concept and define the look of Mercedes-Benz passenger cars. Important design elements are the generously sized horizontal headlamps, the indicators, which can be seen clearly both from the front and the side, the ribbed taillights and the reach-through door handles.

1975

Bruno Sacco succeeds Friedrich Geiger as head of the styling department and thus becomes the new head of design at Mercedes-Benz.

1979

The design of the new S-Class combines traditional elements with new forms that have been developed as part of the aerodynamic optimization process. Defining features include the rising beltline, the integral bumpers and the tapering rear section.

The 126 S-Class created a new view of refinement and responsible engineering.

1982

Mercedes-Benz presents the 190 and 190 E models. The design of the new compact series, which is the forerunner of today's C-Class, represents the consistent continuation of the principles that shaped the S-Class. The rear rises noticeably above the lower beltline of the body. It is a design choice that is initially regarded as somewhat controversial by the public, but is subsequently recognized as a timeless defining feature.

1984

The new W124 medium-size model series has a boot lid with an almost V-shaped rear face, which makes for a low loading sill while maintaining a high-level aerodynamic spoiler lip.

1991

With the new S-Class, Mercedes-Benz also presents a new interpretation of the radiator grille – the defining element of the brand.

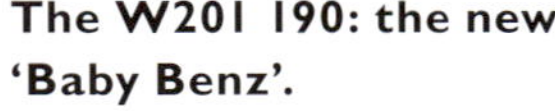

The W201 190: the new 'Baby Benz'.

The V-shape is framed by the taillights and is later picked up by other model series and successor generations as a characteristic styling element.

The new W140 S-Class model has an integrated radiator that is incorporated in the bonnet.

1993

As part of the first major product initiative, the Mercedes-Benz coupé study causes a stir at the Geneva Motor Show. For the first time, Mercedes-Benz presents the C-Class, the successor to the compact class, in four different design and equipment lines. The interior design plays an especially important role in expressing the particular character of the chosen variant.

ABOVE: **The coupé study for the new C-Class.**

LEFT: **The first showing of a completely new interpretation of the Mercedes face with four elliptical headlamps.**

The compact saloon to replace the 201 C-Class.

C-Class interior options add to the sense of integration.

The Designo range of leathers.

The new E-Class Mercedes advertisements referencing the new headlamp style: 'Seeing the Mercedes with new eyes.'

The new W220 S-Class heralded a new elongated style.

1995

The new E-Class is the first series production model with the ground-breaking twin-headlamp face. The new type of front-end design is also adopted in other model series.

The Designo range offers Mercedes-Benz customers with particularly discerning taste countless possibilities for combining exceptional paint finishes, extra-soft leather in exclusive colours and trim elements with surface finishes in fine wood, piano lacquer, stone and leather.

1996/1997

The Mercedes-Benz product initiative sees the advent of numerous new model series, such as the SLK, the CLK, the A-Class and the M-Class. Mercedes-Benz develops innovative design solutions for these fundamentally new vehicle concepts.

1998

The elongated, coupé-like profile of the new S-Class symbolizes the new forward-looking brand image of Mercedes-Benz. New standards are also set by the interior design, which harmonizes perfectly with the sportily elegant lines of the body. It exudes a strong sense of character, lightness and luxury. The side indicators, which have been moved into the mirror housings for the first time, become a defining styling feature.

1999

Professor Peter Pfeiffer succeeds Bruno Sacco as head of design.

Peter Pfeiffer takes over from Bruno Sacco as chief of design.

THE EARLY DAYS OF AUTOMOBILE DESIGN

FROM THE CARRIAGE TO THE FIRST PROPER CAR

In the mid- to late nineteenth century, as industrialization gradually took hold in Europe and north America, huge leaps forward in technology began to spill over into public and domestic life. Engineers, scientists, inventors and mathematicians were changing the face of society and, with the development of steam-powered engines, the world was opening up as never before.

Although vast stretches of railway were being built in earnest across the western world, many people (at least, those who could afford it) still travelled by carriage, pulled by horses or oxen on roads that were both made and unmade, many following ancient paths. It is hardly surprising that, in the early days of the automobile, many of the first 'cars' were built in the tradition of the horse-drawn carriage. It was the only design there was, after all.

For their first car, in 1886, Gottlieb Daimler and his chief designer Wilhelm Maybach mounted an engine into a modified carriage. The standing power unit protruded through the floor of the vehicle in front of the rear seats. A couple of years later, Carl Benz took a different design approach for his first automobile; his three-wheeler was more heavily influenced by the bicycle, with a horizontal single-cylinder engine mounted at the rear.

Daimler and Maybach quickly followed Benz in finding their own design style. In 1889, they presented their elegant two-cylinder wire-wheeled car with tubular frame, which also unmistakably borrowed design elements from bicycle manufacture.

Although Benz and Daimler had undoubtedly taken the first significant steps into the world of automobile design, their stylistic ambitions met with limited enthusiasm initially. With most radical design innovation, it takes some time to

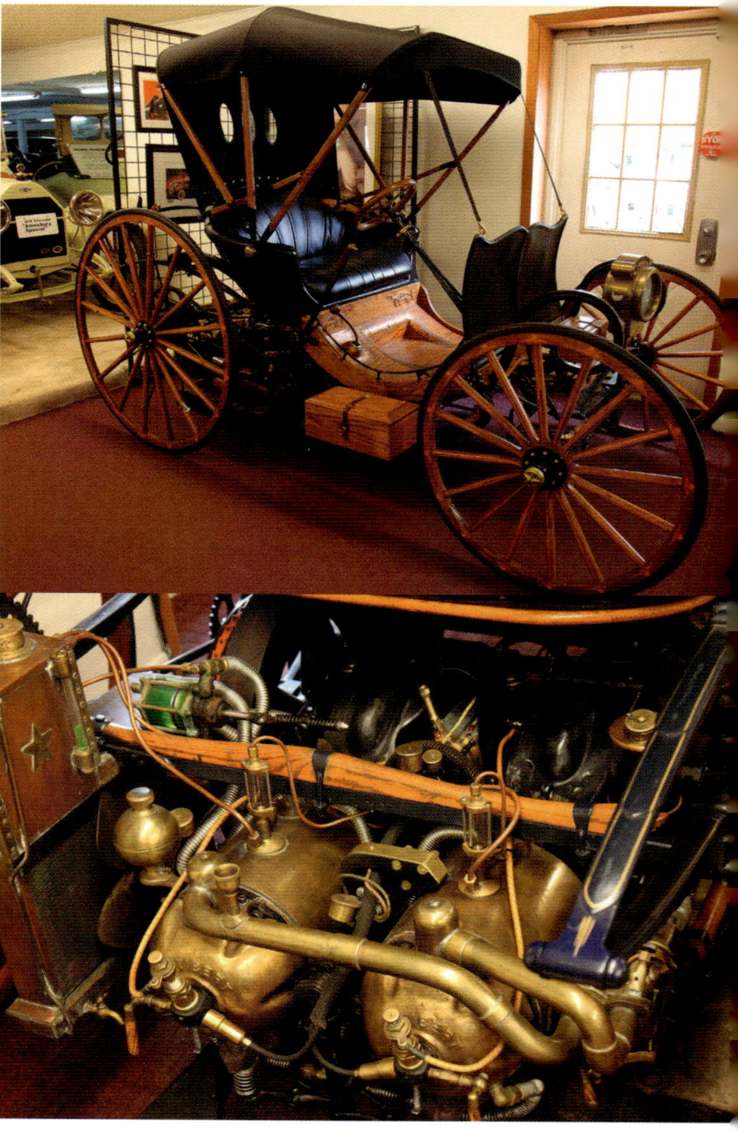

Artisan-built G. Tibert 1892 17 HP.

Lutzmann-built 'horseless carriage' (1895).

An unknown chain-driven carriage from 1896.

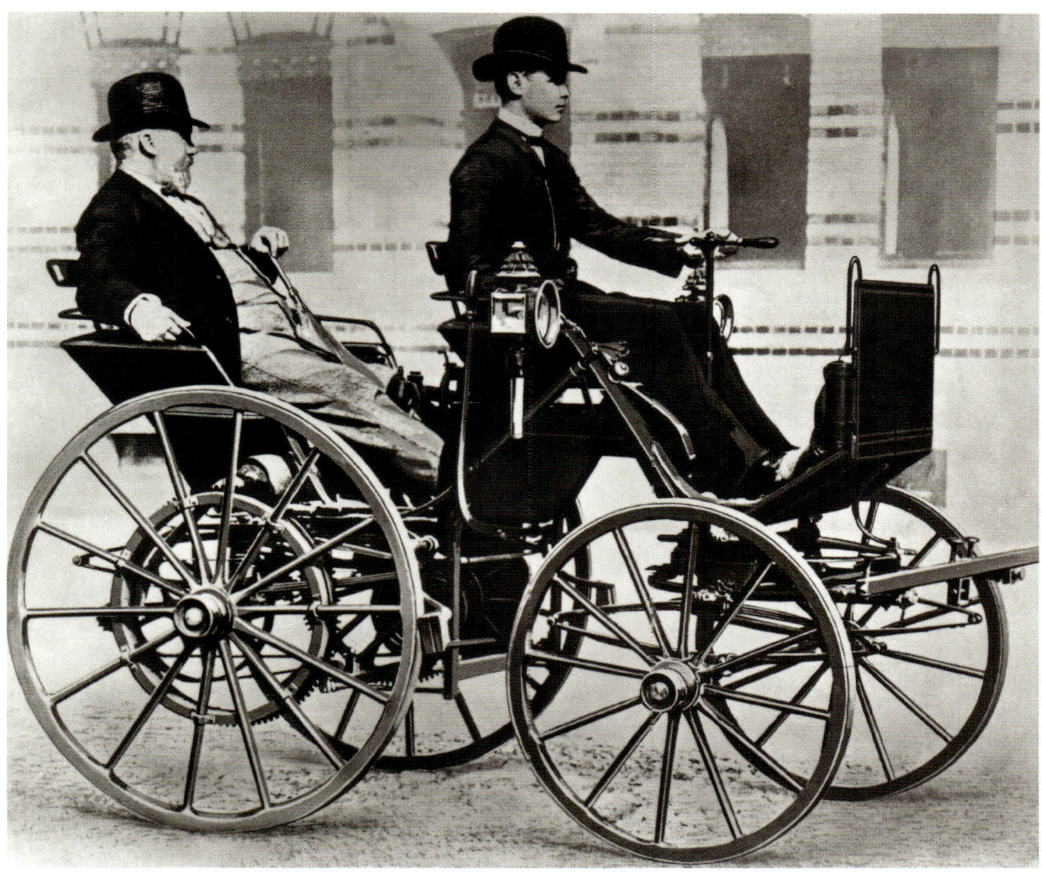

Gottlieb Daimler in the back of his first 'motor carriage', driven by his son Adolf.

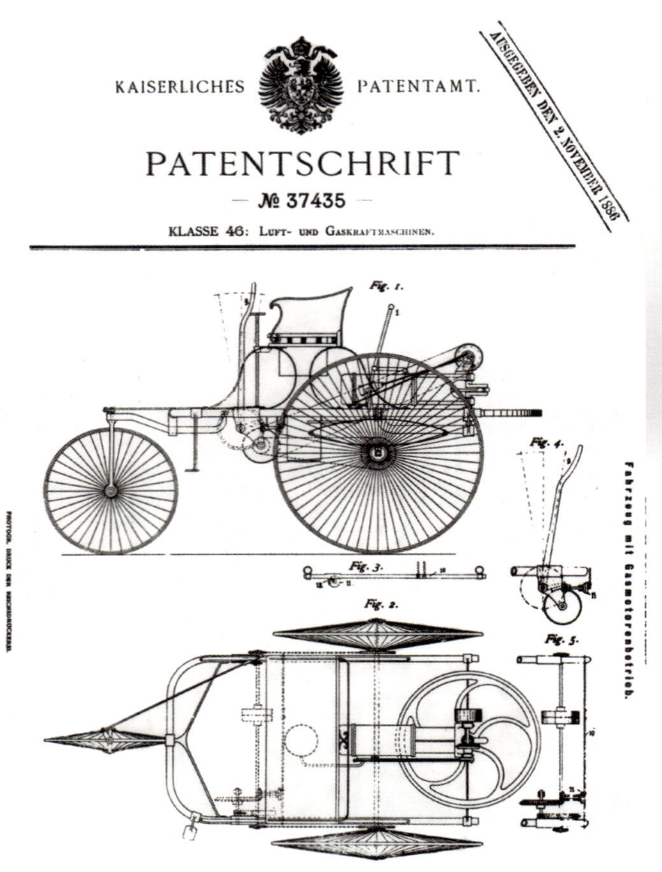

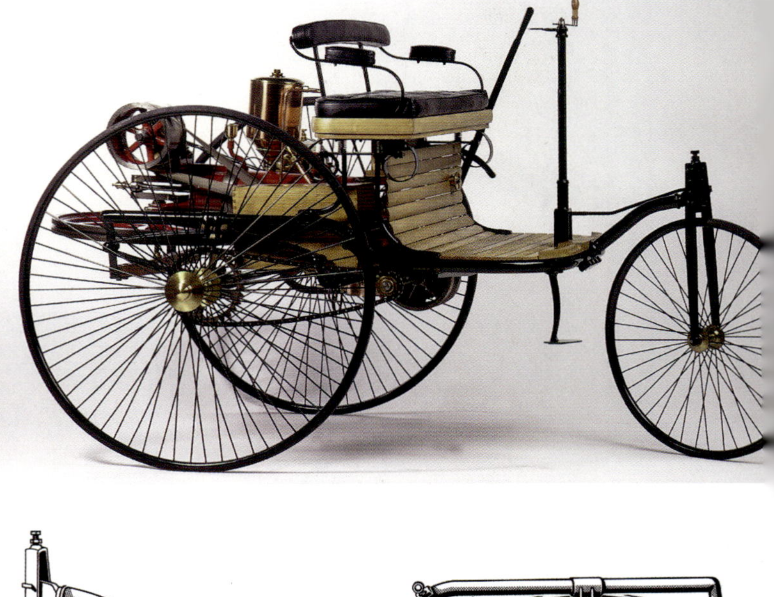

ABOVE: **Carl Benz two-cylinder motor car, with wire wheels, showing the innovative tubular frame.**

LEFT: **Carl Benz patent, 2 November 1886.**

convince enough potential customers of its attributes. For the first time, the developers of the automobile were realizing that it does not matter how innovative a design is; it is the opinion of the customer that keeps a company buoyant.

In simple terms, customers in the late nineteenth century were accustomed to modes of transport looking like a carriage and this is what they expected of the new automobile. At first, both Benz and Daimler were forced to respond to the conservative thinking and returned once again to carriage design. Progress and design had to be paired with conformist thinking.

Perhaps this was no bad thing. A company chronicle produced by Benz in 1910 cited a publication on the subject that dated from the early days of the automobile:

Motor cars can follow the designs of the various customary forms of carriage. When observing the vehicle from the exterior, one notices only the absence of

a drawbar and the extension of the carriage body to the rear. This lengthened carriage body serves to accommodate the driving force, the engine, whereas the drawbar is replaced by a steering stick located in front of the driver's seat.

In order to ensure that the new motor car would appeal to potential customers, Daimler-Motoren-Gesellschaft (Daimler Motors Company, or DMG) – the engineering company that had been founded in 1890 by Daimler and Maybach – needed to convince the public that every horse-drawn carriage could be converted to an automobile by the installation of a motorized mechanism. It was no wonder, then, that carriage design in all its diversity remained the benchmark during the early period.

On 8 March 1886, Gottlieb Daimler ordered a carriage in the 'Americaine' version from coachbuilder Wilhelm Wimpff & Sohn, ostensibly as a present for his wife Emma's

Daimler introduced wire wheels in 1889.

1895 belt-driven two-cylinder.

forthcoming birthday. It became the first commercial 'motor carriage', and it was exactly that – a motorized carriage. It was not until 1889 that Daimler and Maybach were able to move slightly away from conventional carriage technology, by introducing the wire wheel, a two-cylinder engine and a manual gear transmission. It was another small but significant step forward in motor vehicle design.

Even as late as 1897, Daimler's belt-driven cars had remained heavily influenced by carriage design. Handcrafting still dominated and, as such, the early automobiles had no individualistic design styling. The only area where design was a factor at this stage concerned the location of the drive system, and the quest for a sensible solution to this issue would change everything. Most designers were convinced that it was preferable to install the motor behind and below the passenger area. However, when Panhard et Levassor decided to introduce a front-engined car in the early 1890s, the first design challenge (both in terms of concept and construction) arose.

Émile Levassor and René Panhard were great friends of Gottlieb Daimler, and the three engineers often shared information about updates to their vehicles. The Panhard et Levassor concept was adopted by Daimler in 1897; four years later, Carl Benz introduced his first front-engined car.

Despite this important step in functional design, the first front-engined vehicles were still closely modelled on the form of a carriage, with very high ground clearance and a stout appearance. DMG still had to learn that design needed to be more than simply led by function. It took a prototype designed by Paul Daimler (see below), the eldest son of the company founder, as well as a magazine article, to convince them. The article appeared in the *Scientific American* periodical in 1899 and described the Daimler 'Phoenix' as 'a queer-looking thing', with a 'picturesque ugliness'. According to the journalist, it was to be hoped that 'some gifted genius may soon arrive … and whip it into shape and make it a damned sight more presentable!'

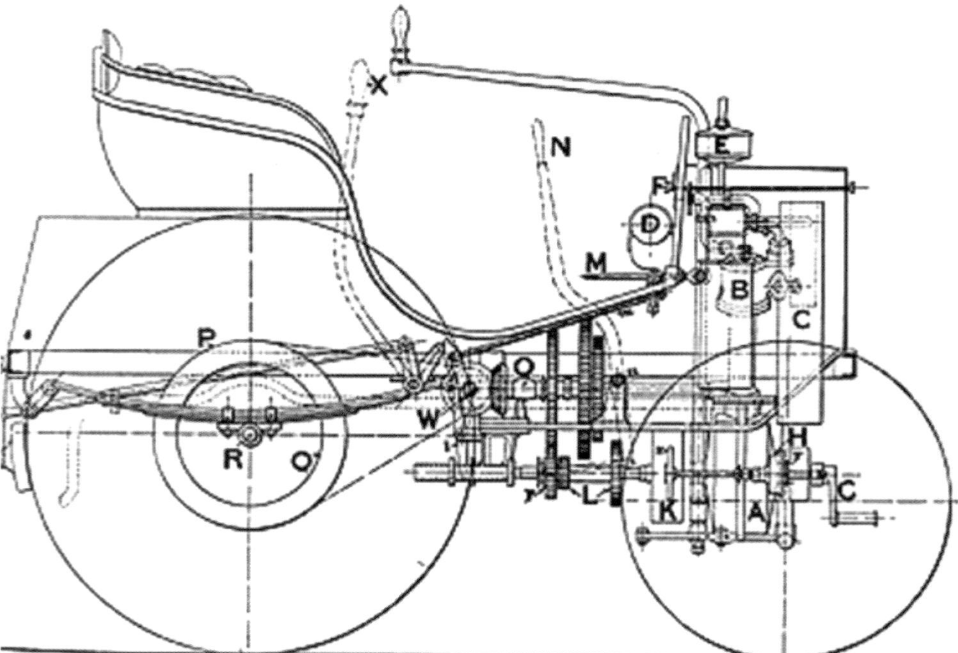

1894 Panhard-Levassor front-engined motor car using a Daimler engine.

1897 'horseless carriage' with optional roof covering.

1897 Daimler Vis à Vis, with a Phoenix engine in the front for the first time.

THE PAUL DAIMLER CAR

Paul Daimler, the eldest son of the company founder, worked in the design office of DMG from 1897 onwards. The young Daimler often considered Wilhelm Maybach's design concepts to be in competition with their own, and was not best pleased when Daimler senior overruled him. After a few run-ins with Maybach, Paul was given his own independent design office.

Having spent his formative years around Panhard and Levassor, Paul was familiar with the compact 'voiturettes', which had become hugely popular in France. He sensed that it would be possible to gain access to this market segment with a modern DMG design. At the end of October 1900, he completed the drawings and passed them on to the workshop.

Although three prototypes were built, the 'Paul Daimler Car', as it was known internally, did not go into mass production. There was a view that it would have been too appealing, to the detriment of the Mercedes models designed by Maybach. In addition, Mercedes sales had been so successful that the DMG production lines were at full capacity. However, alongside the Maybach/Mercedes, the Paul Daimler Car had shown clearly that design was not just about function; it could also represent innovation and identity.

Daimler junior went on to develop some very good engineering strategies, especially after the death of his father. He and Maybach managed to work alongside and support one another, even under the strain of the DMG board.

The Emil Jellinek 'first modern car'.

Paul Daimler's car never saw production.

Daimler Phoenix car, 1898–1902, with the engine at the front and a four-speed gearbox.

THE FIRST MERCEDES MODEL SERIES

The development of highly sports-oriented vehicles in the period from 1899 to 1901 resulted in significant stylistic changes. With the production of its first Mercedes, DMG succeeded in making the leap from carriage-like vehicles to the first proper car.

The idea behind the 35 HP vehicle came originally at the turn of the century from Emil Jellinek, a diplomat and businessman who was based in Nice on the French Riviera. Jellinek was DMG's main agent and distributor in the south of France, selling their cars under his company name of 'Mercedes', and he would often advise DMG on what they should be producing. He had already enjoyed success with DMG cars in events at the Riviera 'speed week', but in 1900

Mercedes 35 HP designed by Emil Jellinek.

The first motor car with a honeycomb radiator was also the first with the name 'Mercedes' marked on it in script, in honour of Emil Jellinek's daughter.

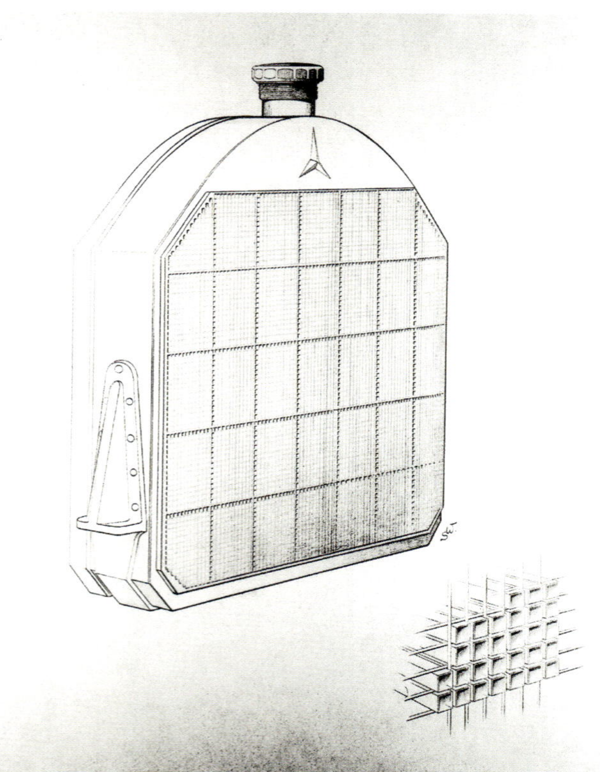

The honeycomb radiator, designed by Wilhelm Maybach in 1896.

he urged Wilhelm Maybach, chief designer at DMG in Bad Cannstatt, to build a new car that would be even more powerful. The first Mercedes was therefore a car designed for motorsport. Differing so radically from other automobiles of the day, and with such innovative engineering details, the 35 HP Mercedes represented a final move away from carriage design. It is regarded today as the first modern automobile.

One of the highlights of the car's design was the honeycomb radiator, which was designed by Maybach and made a definite breakthrough in the solution of the cooling problem. The use of small tubes of rectangular rather than round cross-section allowed for considerably improved cooling efficiency, due to the larger surface area and the smaller gaps between the tubes. The honeycomb radiator not only paved the way functionally for the high-performance reliable automobile, but also gave the vehicle a distinctive new face.

The innovative design of the first Mercedes was subsequently used as a blueprint by other manufacturers. At the Paris Motor Show of December 1902, there were so many Mercedes imitators that the press labelled the event 'Salon Mercedes'. They also rightly referred to the racing and sports car designed by Wilhelm Maybach as the 'first modern car'.

The appearance and influence of the Mercedes car was described in an early DMG chronicle:

The most striking thing about the outward appearance of this car was its low and elongated design, the sharply canted steering column and typical Mercedes radiator grille. This model was responsible for revolutionizing the automotive industry in every country.

Italian automobile designer Bruno Sacco, the legendary head of styling at Daimler-Benz from the 1970s to the 1990s, saw in the 35 HP Mercedes not only a masterpiece of technical beauty, but also the basis of Mercedes-Benz design history:

The design was not only technologically thought through and stylistically unique; it also proved to be extremely successful. It laid the foundations for a new era in automotive design.

DESIGNING FOR COMFORT AND SAFETY

Having its own body design and building department provided DMG with a great business opportunity, as new ways of thinking about vehicle design developed. Other automotive manufacturers had their own chassis and engine configurations but were now commissioning DMG to build their bodies for them. As time went on, there was a growing demand for a bespoke service. Although function and innovation remained the driving forces behind design, customers also began to embrace the latest trends and the desire for fashionable features began to influence design.

Compared with the horse and cart, the automobile posed completely new challenges in terms of design. Gottlieb Daimler and Carl Benz may have invented this new mode of transport independently of one other, in 1886, but initially they followed different paths. Benz developed a patent motor car based on a bicycle with wire wheels, while Daimler's was a motorized carriage. However, nothing could stop the rapid progression in technology, or the rise in customer expectations, and their automobiles had to be adapted to accommodate new demands. The challenge was to achieve greater comfort and greater speeds, without endangering other road users. The feature that had to change first was the chassis.

In 1889, Wilhelm Maybach, the brilliant design engineer working alongside Daimler, developed the steel-wheeled car and, at the same time, a chassis divorced from carriage-building techniques. There were also major strides in the development

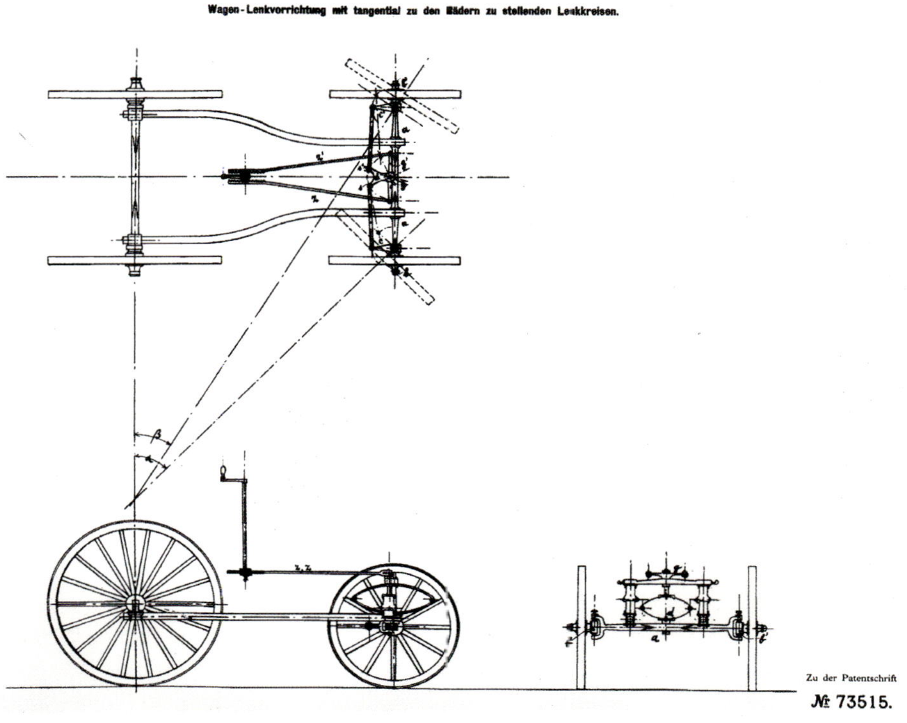

Having come across this patent when browsing through a trade journal in 1891, Carl Benz realized its significance for automobile design. The specification that 'the extended lines of the wheel axes must converge in the centre point of the bend' helped him to develop double-pivot steering.

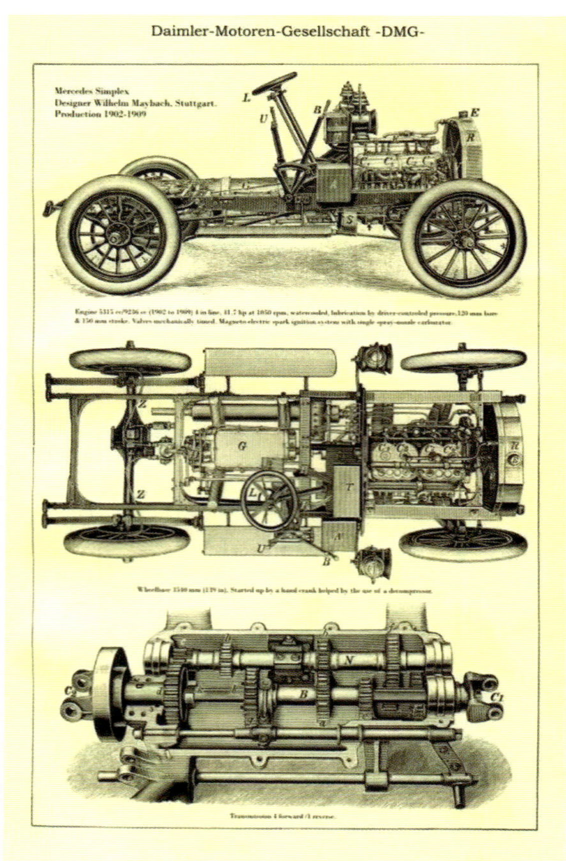

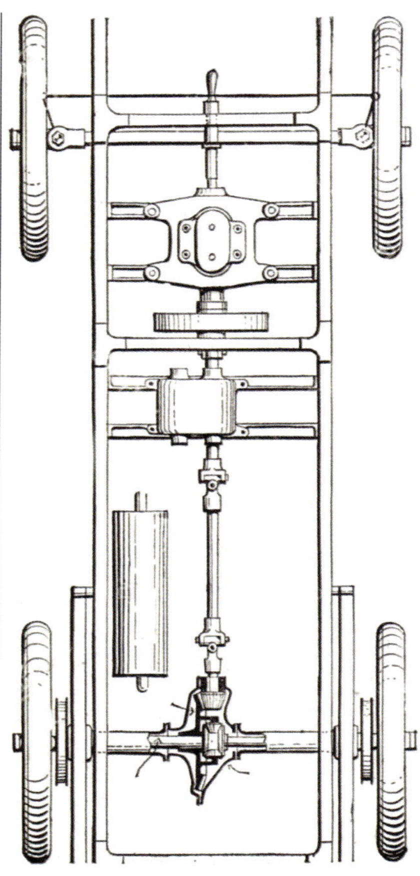

The DMG direct-drive 'Cardan' series.

opment of increasingly powerful engines. Vehicles became faster, but they were also heavier, posing new challenges for the chassis engineers. The design solutions included coil springs, which were installed in 1895 on the rear axle of the Daimler belt-drive car, and double-pivot steering, which was introduced by Gottlieb Daimler to solve the problem of how to pilot a four-wheeled vehicle. In 1893, Benz patented this innovative steering, which was first used on the 'Victoria' model.

After the turn of the century, the universal driveshaft finally took over from the chain drive. It was installed in the Benz 'Parsifal', which appeared in 1902 as the response to the Mercedes 'Simplex'. The universal driveshaft required a complete modification of the rear axle. The axle gearing gained an integral differential gear, which increased the unsprung masses. As this required more rear axle damping, additional dampers were installed.

Chassis engineering received a major innovative boost in the 1930s as road surfaces improved significantly, mak-

ing them better suited to faster traffic. Punctures occurred less frequently and the chassis structures were safer and more comfortable. Particularly important was the additional front-wheel brake, which appeared for the first time in Mercedes series production cars in 1921, initially in the powerful 28/95 PS sports model. From the summer of 1924, all Mercedes passenger cars were fitted with brakes on all four wheels. The invention of the shock absorber made passenger cars, which were still overwhelmingly fitted with rigid axles and leaf springs, considerably more comfortable, even if this aspect still left much to be desired, especially in the smaller and lighter vehicles.

At the 1931 Paris Motor Show, the Mercedes-Benz 170 showed off a completely novel chassis with independent axles, representing a significant milestone in the direction of ride comfort and driving safety. The front wheels of this vehicle's four individually suspended wheels were hung with no axle from a transverse-mounted pair of leaf springs. Each of the rear wheels was suspended from a semi-swing axle

The first swing axle made its appearance on the teardrop race car in 1923.

A clear view of leaf springs.

whose jacket tubes were each anchored to the frame by two coil springs on the wheel side and to the differential by pivot bearings. The result was a great reduction in the proportion of unsprung masses.

Individual wheel suspension, installed in every Mercedes-Benz passenger car since its introduction in the 170 'Max-ime' model, gained the company a reputation for building extraordinarily comfortable and safe vehicles.

The Mercedes-Benz 170 was followed in 1933 by the 380 model eight-cylinder compressor sports car, another vehicle with fully independent suspension, whose front wheels were suspended for the first time from parallelogram trans-

Independent front suspension of the Mercedes-Benz 170 (W15) of 1931, with two transverse-mounted leaf springs and hydraulic shock absorbers.

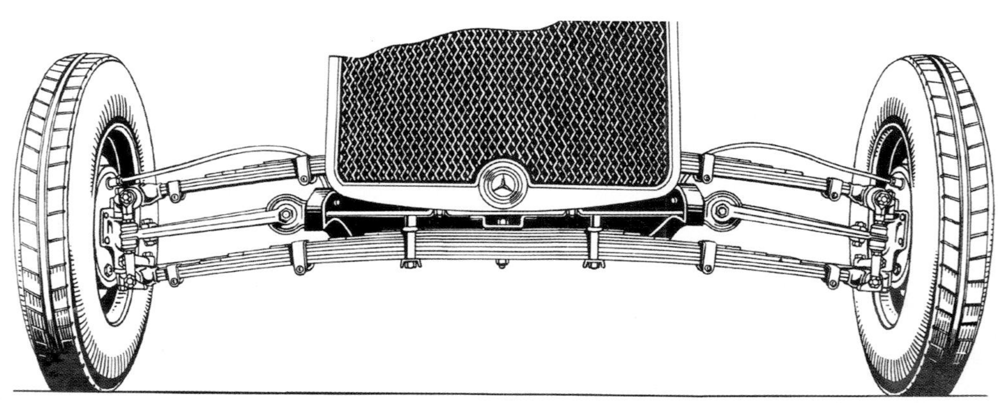

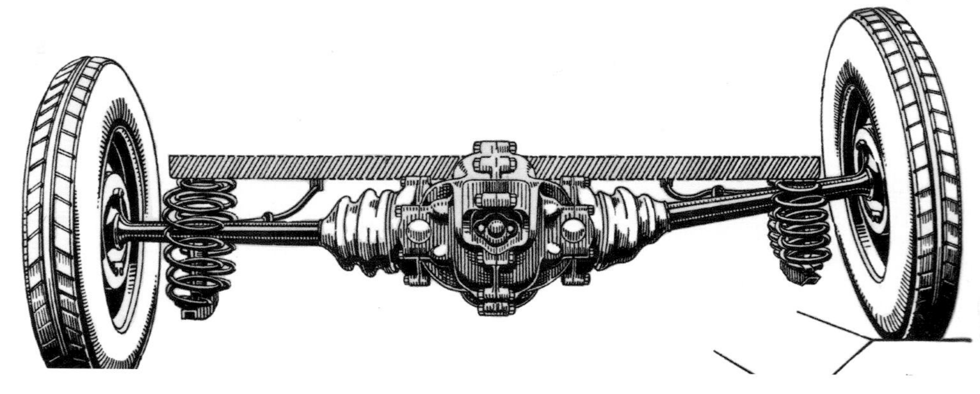

Independent coil springs on the rear of the 170 improved comfort and road-holding enormously.

verse control arms with coil springs. This pioneering design, which treated wheel control, suspension and damping as separate systems, became the standard front suspension, not just for Mercedes-Benz but for numerous other manufacturers throughout the world.

After various refinements, the two-joint swing axle, as introduced in 1931 in the Type 170 model, eventually became the single-joint swing axle in 1954. It would continue unchanged as a standard Mercedes-Benz component until 1972. It, too, had thrust arms and coil springs, with an additional horizontal compensating coil spring on the more powerful models.

A new era in ride comfort was opened up by a variant introduced in 1961. Initially available with the Mercedes-Benz 300 SE, it featured air chamber spring bellows replacing the coil springs; at the same time, hydro-pneumatic self-levelling was introduced for the rear axle. This was a development from a self-levelling control system that had appeared earlier on, in 1951, on the Mercedes-Benz 300, operated via an electrically selectable torsion bar spring. The Mercedes-Benz 600 even had shock absorbers whose characteristics could be adjusted from inside the vehicle.

The next significant step was the diagonal swing axle that was introduced in 1968 in the 114/115 model series. The design was based on a semi-trailing arm axle which was also supported on coil springs, ensuring that track and, in particular, camber remained largely constant under spring compression and rebound.

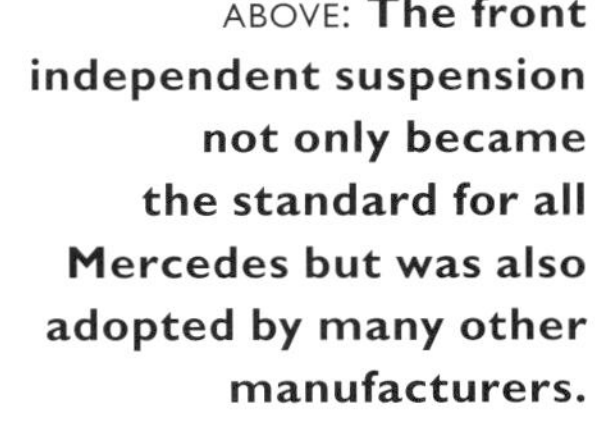

ABOVE: **The front independent suspension not only became the standard for all Mercedes but was also adopted by many other manufacturers.**

Single joint swing axle from a W100 600. This set-up was used well into the 1970s.

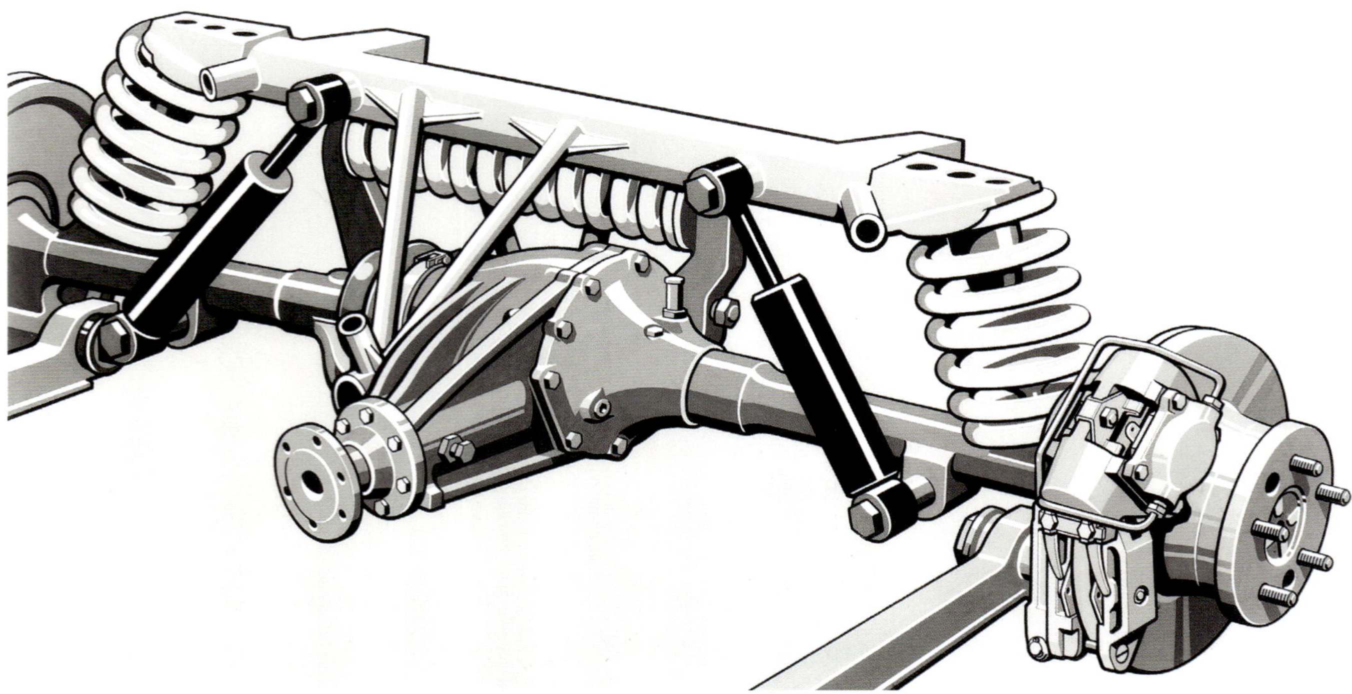

Diagonal swing axle.

The end of 1982 saw the introduction of the Mercedes-Benz 190 in the W201 compact class series. It was the direct forerunner of the C-Class. Its unprecedented multi-link independent rear suspension was a technical sensation. The optimal travel of the independently suspended rear wheels was achieved by distributing the forces and moments to five three-dimensionally arranged links, the geometry of each being especially tailored to its function. Comfort and road-holding were optimized independently of each other. All this was complemented by an equally redesigned front suspension on transverse control arms with damper struts and separately located coil springs. The multi-link independent rear suspension was gradually introduced into the other Mercedes-Benz models.

DESIGNING FOR AESTHETICS

The second decade of the twentieth century brought with it major changes. Einstein published his general theory of relativity, the first all-metal aeroplane took to the air, as did the Zeppelin. With the Trans-Siberian Railway linking the west with Vladivostok and the Panama Canal drastically shortening the route between the Atlantic and Pacific oceans, the world was becoming smaller.

Before the First World War, automotive design centred primarily on technology. Master bodybuilders determined the structure and lines of the first cars based on little more than functionality; the idea that the shape of a car should, could or would involve a designers or an artist never entered the mind of any manufacturer.

On the art scene, however, Futurism and, later, Aestheticism were making waves. These movements idealized technology and the artistic perspective soon had an impact on real automotive design. For example, wing designs began to be drawn to represent speed and dynamism; the wing now had an aesthetic role as well as a functional one. No longer did form simply 'follow function'; on the contrary, many automotive companies and bodybuilders used elements that were clearly designed to arouse emotions. Pioneers such as Walter Gropius (the architect and founder of the Bauhaus movement) enthused over the beauty of the car and many proposed automotive design sketches of their own. As the body of the car began to be designed more in line with aesthetic principles, the growing number of technical designers now also became

THE BLITZEN-BENZ

For Benz & Cie, the Blitzen-Benz of 1909 became the first vehicle to embody a dynamic appearance with a cohesive design idiom. A famous racing and record-breaking machine, it became the first land-going vehicle to pass the 200km/h mark, and set a new land speed record at Daytona Beach in 1911 of 141.7mph.

The Blitzen-Benz was the first vehicle to be designed taking aerodynamic considerations specifically into account. Although aerodynamics had no very significant role to play for the road vehicles at the time, the Blitzen-Benz set new standards in the evolution of the automobile. Rather than being separated from the body at the firewall, the chassis with the engine and front structure were integrated with it in a formal unit. This design feature began to be adopted on passenger cars, although this change occurred gradually, because of the greater width of the body of the vehicles. The 'torpedo' became a defining design feature. Also referred to as a 'cowl', the bulge below the windscreen provided a formal link between the engine box and the body.

The new flat sidewalls and continuous waistline meant that the separate entities of chassis, engine housing and body began to be fused into one organic unit, presenting a new challenge for body design.

The Blitzen-Benz, with its teardrop aerodynamics.

It was on the Blitzen-Benz that body design became one fluid unit for the first time.

stylists. These were the people who became responsible for automotive design gradually developing what would become the typical car shape of the future.

Expressing Brand Value

In subsequent years, the lines of Mercedes-Benz automobiles continued to capture the imagination of the public. Their innovative approach was seen to reflect both the

ABOVE: **Mercedes-Benz's race pedigree raised awareness of brand values.**

philosophy and the status of the brand. It was design that raised awareness of the product while also expressing the brand values.

A DMG chronicle made the following observations during this period:

> *The boom in German industry and German trade brought money into the country and this money changed hands briskly. The hard-working business ethic brought a prosperity that manifested itself in a certain desire for luxury.*
>
> *The automotive manufacturers sensed this also and sought to meet this need by producing particularly refined vehicle bodies. If we compare Mercedes vehicles of earlier years with those of subsequent years we see the tangible expression of this desire for luxury embodied in ever more elegant forms.*
>
> *In the place of the ugly rear-entry tonneau come side-entry vehicles with a closed roof. The vehicles become longer and lower, with doors for entry and greater protection for passengers and drivers.*

A book about Benz automobiles, published in 1910, adds the following:

The 10/25 HP Benz landaulet of 1912, showing the slightly raked screen and integrated body.

**Mercedes saloon
22/50 HP, 1915.**

The latest bodies produced at the Benz factories attach particular importance to closed, rounded lines and gentle, gradual transitions between the various elements of the car. This helps on the one hand to reduce wind resistance as far as possible, and on the other lends the motor car the appearance of a harmoniously designed and integrated whole.

Examples of this modern styling are the 22/50 HP Mercedes of 1915 and the 10/25 HP Benz of 1912. The sales brochure for the 10/25 HP Benz, which Benz offered ex-factory as a four-seater runabout model, two-seater sports car, open and closed landaulet and a limousine, confidently alluded to the 'now generally preferred all-enclosed form'.

The brochure went on to emphasize the car's appealing look and the level of comfort it would offer:

The lines continue uninterrupted from the bonnet via the windscreen and along the side walls to the front seats. The entire body of the car, with its casual lines and heavily canted steering column, lends the vehi-cle a sporty appearance. An adjustable glass plate mounted ahead of the front seats serves to prevent draughts. Small electric lanterns are integrated into the wind deflector.

The practical American soft top roof, which can be put up quickly and simply, offers protection from the elements and when folded down can be safely stowed beneath a dust cover.

Increasingly, references were made in the marketing material to interior comfort and spaciousness, the use of high-quality materials and meticulous interior design. 'Exquisite taste' was highly praised. Craftsmanship was in demand.

The Trademark Radiator

Throughout the first forty years of automotive history, the radiator grille fulfilled a purely practical function — it was designed to stop the engine from overheating and to keep it at an optimal temperature. Its shape was purely the result of

The mighty chain-driven 37/90 HP.

applying practical engineering reasoning and was certainly not seen by car manufacturers as a way of personalizing their brand.

The late 1800s and early 1900s saw a series of long-distance rallies in Europe, with open-road racing, often from city to city. In 1908, automobile enthusiast Prinz Heinrich of Prussia set up an international touring event, open to four-seater cars that were licensed for use on public roads. Having entered the first Prinz Heinrich Rally, Benz & Cie soon identified the fact that winning was all about maintaining a high constant speed. Many of the stages were designed for flat-out racing and, by 1910, competitors were beginning to look for cars that had more streamlined bodies.

One solution came from Paul Daimler, then chief designer at DMG. He equipped the Mercedes vehicles with a sharply pointed radiator grille, resembling the bow of a ship. It was designed to cut through the air, thereby reducing aerodynamic drag. At the same time, its greater surface area offered improved cooling over the flat radiator with similar cross-section. Manufacturing such a radiator was not easy, however, which may explain why other car manufacturers initially seemed reluctant to copy the design. Although Mercedes did not win every

time, the principle of the pointed radiator nevertheless proved its worth.

In 1911, DMG introduced a new sports car with the characteristic pointed radiator grille and external exhaust pipes. This was the mighty, chain-driven 37/90 HP. The same features were also exhibited a short time later on the 28/95 HP six-cylinder. This representative saloon went down in corporate history as the most elegant automobile of the period, and it was built until 1924, ensuring that the pointed radiator grille continued into the post-war era.

For DMG, the pointed radiator styling represented a new and significant design, and the birth of one Mercedes trademark. It did not, however, feature on all vehicles produced by the world's oldest carmaker. In 1926 Daimler and Benz merged to become Daimler-Benz AG, the model range was restructured and vehicles were offered under the brand name of Mercedes-Benz. The large six-cylinder, supercharged vehicles were equipped with the pointed radiator, but the new 8/38 HP and 12/55 HP models, as well as the eight-cylinder Nürburg of 1928, were given a flat radiator, to identify them as smaller cars. Clearly, there had been a leap in understanding that design is not just about shape, but can also define a class of vehicle.

Mercedes 28/95 HP, constructed in 1924.

Mercedes Benz Type 170V, showing its canted radiator style.

By the middle of the 1930s, many car manufacturers had recognized that the image of their brand could be strongly associated with their radiator design. A distinctive front end was often used to emphasize the sense of belonging to a brand. The designers at Mercedes-Benz chose to retain the traditional shape, adapting it almost imperceptibly and taking great care before making any changes to the vehicle's overall shape. This adherence to the traditional visual symbol proved a significant competitive advantage for the brand.

The first Mercedes radiators stood up tall and straight against the oncoming wind. In 1937, the radiator grille on the Mercedes-Benz Type 170V retained the high, streamlined basic form, but it was tilted backwards slightly, as a clear visual reflection of the vehicle's exceptional dynamics. This basic stylistic configuration continued until the 1960s. At that time, the Mercedes-Benz radiator became wider and lower, in accordance with the trend of making bonnets flatter, in order to meet aerodynamic needs.

Although the typical Mercedes front has undergone many changes over the years, it has always remained an unmistakable and characteristic feature.

THE THREE-POINTED STAR

Automotive manufacturers were well aware that design principles were often the subject of imitation and DMG realized that the addition of a distinctive symbol was the only way in which its vehicles could be identified with absolute certainty. Even before the company moved to Untertürkheim, in 1904, DMG had furnished some vehicles with the initials 'DC', for Daimler Cannstatt. Later on, an oval badge was mounted on the radiator grille bearing the name 'Mercedes'.

In 1909, the chairman of the supervisory board of DMG, Alfred von Kaulla, decided that the company must have a definitive symbol. Eventually, DMG opted for the three-pointed star, perhaps recalling the symbol that Gottlieb Daimler had once drawn to mark the location of his house on a postcard to his wife. The three points are said to represent land, sea and air, and the company's ambition to provide motorization in all three environments. In that same year, the first three-pointed stars appeared at the front of the Mercedes radiator grille.

THE ROARING TWENTIES

Following the devastation of the First World War, Europe had to find its way again. Alongside the development of new socio-political theories in the 1920s, tougher industrial competition, and artists seeking modern forms of expression, there was a resurgent sense of optimism. In the field of technology, new visions were being explored. Hermann Julius Oberth published a book on the construction of interplanetary rockets and at the AVUS in Berlin Fritz Opel tested a rocket-powered racing car.

During this time, the automobile was subject to a raft of further developments. For decades, the automotive body form had been dominated by the open touring car, which had naturally derived from the carriage. However, it was the saloon style that now began to prevail, even for smaller, self-driven vehicles.

This trend for the 'closed-in form' once again presented body designers with particular challenges. It was much more difficult to create beautiful, well-proportioned flowing lines than it had been on an open-top vehicle, and the very early saloon bodies were generally rather angular in appearance. Oddly though, as the decade progressed, the 'open-driving' design re-emerged, but this time it was offered in a combination of the two styles: the optimum protection offered by the saloon combined with a luxuriously padded, robust and yet easy-to-use soft top with side windows, which could be mounted and closed to create a hermetic seal. Unsurprisingly, these 'convertibles' were generally the most expensive variants offered by automotive manufacturers and bodybuilders.

From around 1929 onwards, stylists discovered that gentle flowing lines gave off dynamic visual cues that attracted the public in general as well as potential customers. Although the wings had been shaped, thus far, only to fulfil their function as mudguards, body designers now began to give them more sweeping lines. This gave the vehicle character and evoked elegance, speed and comfort. In addition, the lines could also reflect styles in contemporary art.

Mercedes vehicles had adopted a number of design features from the pre-war period and carried these through into the 1930s: the three-pointed-star, the pointed radiator and the external exhaust pipes. According to one historian, 'A Mercedes of the early 1920s was unmistakably German with its proud, pointed radiator grille and tall body sides – a homage to its predecessors, the mighty and highly successful racing vehicles that won the French Grand Prix of 1914.'

The 8/38 HP Mercedes-Benz of 1926 was the first vehicle built by the Mercedes-Benz brand. It was available in several closed and open variants, and as a four-seater, four-door convertible. The saloon was relatively angular and featured a luggage compartment attached to the rear. Apart from a flat radiator grille with a Mercedes star mounted above it, the dominant features were its flowing wings, which merged with the running boards to form a single visual entity.

In this decade of upheaval, Daimler-Benz AG also introduced the famous Mercedes-Benz SS/SSKL (1927–1932). Today, these models are considered iconic classics, whose proportions alone symbolize pedigree and athleticism. One distinctive feature of these fast top-of-the-range models, which Mercedes-Benz positioned in the segment for luxury sports vehicles, was the face. This was dominated by a mighty, upright, slightly pointed chrome-plated honeycomb radiator, usually protected at the front by an elegant grille in close-ribbed herringbone pattern. Outsized headlamps

Mercedes-Benz Type 8/38 HP limousine, 1926.

The 1926 SS Sportwagen 27/140 cabriolet.

attached to the still traditional headlamp bar alongside the radiator ensured adequate long-distance illumination for driving. The body, which was joined to the imposing engine cowling and emphasized the vehicle's length, had a comparatively low waistline and freestanding wings.

These exciting vehicles also featured external exhaust pipes, first introduced before the First World War, which protruded from the sides of the engine cowling. Although it was imitated by other manufacturers, this emotive and sporty design feature remained a trademark of Mercedes-Benz supercharged vehicles until the 1940s, and has been echoed in the modern era on the Mercedes-Benz SLR McLaren.

The S, SS and SSK models were considered ideals of beauty in their day – they were what the public believed a 'proper car' should look like. For the lucky driver, equipped with the obligatory dust jacket, leather cap and protective goggles, an excursion in such a car was a highly intense and immediate experience. More importantly, these sports cars notched up numerous victories on international racetracks between 1927 and 1932. As such, they were the first ambassadors for the company, earning valuable publicity and communicating Mercedes-Benz's brand values to the entire world. Outstanding design had become a Mercedes-Benz trademark.

The Mercedes-Benz SSK (1928–1932) was one of the world's most popular high-performance sports cars.

June 1927: Rudolf Caracciola wins the opening race of the then brand-new Nürburgring. The Mercedes-Benz S (as in 'sport') was the first of a whole range of legendary high-performance sports cars to dominate the racing circuits.

THE 'SINDELFINGEN BODY'

The 1920s and 1930s were a time of upheaval for the automotive industry. Manufacturers were attempting to distance themselves further and further from classic body shapes that were often still rooted in the coach and carriage era. Those customers who could afford it would have their own, individual vehicle built, and this was made possible by the concept of a chassis construction with a separate body set on top. The service was offered by numerous bodybuilding companies, who would simply order the chassis and equip it with a body to meet the customer's requirements. This form of individualization was a lucrative business, which the manufacturers were gradually discovering for themselves.

Daimler-Benz AG set up its special vehicle production unit in the Sindelfingen plant in 1932. Before its establishment, specialized customer requirements had been met by third-party bodybuilders, but the Sindelfingen plant – and the Mercedes-Benz brand – soon earned itself a reputation for putting wheels under some rather unusual one-off creations. The 'Sindelfinger Karosserie' badge, mounted on the left-hand side of the vehicle, became synonymous with unusual vehicle bodies built to the highest standards of quality and craftsmanship.

The plant manager in Sindelfingen from January 1932 was Dr Wilhelm Haspel, a commercially trained engineer. His aim in establishing the special unit was to prevent the time-consuming manual craftsmanship involved in producing special bodies disrupting the production flow of the series-produced models. Furthermore, the set-up allowed Daimler-Benz to respond to even the most elaborate of customer requests, and to earn money by doing so. It was income that Haspel did not want to relinquish without a fight.

Hermann Ahrens was appointed as the manager of the unit, having been persuaded to take on the task by the trio at the top of the company: Haspel, Wilhelm Kissel (chairman of the board) and Dr Hans Nibel (board member for development). Ahrens had previously been responsible for the design of exclusive models for the Horch Company, a role which had brought him to the attention of the management team at Mercedes-Benz.

To begin with, the structure of the production unit was unclear. In April 1933, Ahrens was joined by Friedrich Geiger. Both Ahrens and Geiger considered themselves to be engineers and not simply designers – their role encompassed both the styling and its constructive implementation, a concept that reflects rather more the Anglo-Saxon understanding of the term 'design'.

Mannheim body workshop.

The revered 'Sindelfingen Karosserie' badge.

Mercedes-Benz 500K Special Streamliner (W29) from 1935, destined for a customer from the Dutch East Indies.

The shape of the body represents an interim stage between the 500K Autobahnkurier ('Autobahn courier') and the uncompromisingly aerodynamic 540K Streamliner of 1938.

The economic recovery that had begun in 1932, and then took stronger hold from 1933 on, brought with it a growing interest in exclusive vehicles and thus in the special vehicle production unit. It was here that the many different versions of the supercharged models 380 (W22), 500K and 540K (W29), as well as the Grand Mercedes (W07 and W150), were built, featuring what were often very complicated special requests.

Between 1932 and 1939, a whole range of elaborate body shells for both open and enclosed vehicles were built in Sindelfingen, along with bodies fitted with special protection. Many of the elegantly designed bodies produced during that period under the aegis of Ahrens and Geiger have a timeless beauty about them. Even decades later, they have lost nothing of their fascination or radiance. Quite a few of the vehicles of that time regularly receive awards today in renowned

Mercedes-Benz 320 (W142) Streamliner saloon, 1938.

540K cabriolet produced in 1936 or the 540K with fully aerodynamic body that was supplied to the German Dunlop works in 1938.

Concours d'Élégance, such as that held at Pebble Beach in California every year. Right at the top of the list of these design highlights stands the Special Roadster, with its raked radiator grille, which still takes to the public stage to enthusiastic applause on a regular basis. The cabriolet variants of the same model, with their snugly fitting, lined soft tops, have the added advantage of greater everyday practicality. Sindelfingen also produced the first cabriolet models with a hard top, aptly known as 'combination cars' or 'combination coupés'.

The unit at Sindelfingen accommodated all sorts of individual requests from customers: special chrome adornment in the form of a protective grille in front of the pointed radiator, or chrome strips emphasizing the vehicle's elegant lines; two spare wheels within the front wings or in the rear of the vehicle, which had a significant impact on the design of the body; or the addition of such equipment items as a radiator or a heater. Some of the features may be taken for granted today, but back then they were exclusive optional extras.

Wherever possible, the special vehicle production unit would turn the dreams of its discerning clientele into reality. Ahrens reported that it was not unusual for the family of the future vehicle owner to visit for a few days, in order to discuss and choose the body shape, to make their individual selection of colours and materials, and to determine the technical specification. The result in each case would be a unique vehicle, tailored perfectly to an individual lifestyle.

The expertise and flexibility of the specialists in Sindelfingen meant that they also became involved in constructing the extremely lightweight bodies that needed to be built at short notice for sporting use in the popular off-road races of the 1930s. some of the aluminium-bodied two-seater models created at the unit weighed barely 100kg. Special requests from potential customers for aerodynamically designed bodies found a sympathetic ear among the bodybuilding artists. They shied away from nothing, not even from the otherwise seemingly untouchable pointed radiator.

1933–1949: THE DARK YEARS

In Germany, Adolf Hitler's rise to power would shape Europe and the world for more than a decade. In the aftermath of the Second World War, politicians struggled to establish a new world order, but science and technology continued to develop. As before, the car remained for most people an object of luxury or a sporting accessory. This fact influenced the developers and stylists of the 1930s, who continued to strive for forms that reflected not only elegance and sportiness but also opulence and affluence.

Mercedes-Benz 500K 'Autobahn courier', 1934.

In 1934, the Autobahn-Kurierwagen ('motorway cruiser') epitomized modern mobility on four wheels, capable of covering long distances at high speed and in comfort. Four cars were produced based on the 500K and two on the 540K. The curved wings had a drop-shaped and streamlined design, and the rear wings covered the wheels.

After the muscular, masculine lines of the 1920s there was now a desire for gentler, flowing forms with rounded elements. In order to achieve this, the designers merged components that had previously been distinct from one another. First and foremost, this applied to the wings, which now increasingly formed a single entity with the running board. Depending on body type and customer demand, a luggage rack with accompanying suitcases might be mounted on the rear deck, while some vehicles were even equipped with a proper luggage compartment, complete with elegant, hand-made cases.

Design professor Othmar Wickenheiser described the developmental stages as follows:

By around 1930 the luggage compartment had become an integrated part of the body's horizontally subdivided box elements. The surfaces of the wings were cambered.

By 1935 the luggage compartment and spare wheel had become integral components of a two-box split in body proportions. Volumes were markedly rounded in form and the wings now became volume elements with a design defined as teardrop shaped.

By the late 1930s, the continuous shoulder line caused the overall horizontal proportions to develop into a more vertical layout, comprised of lower body and vehicle cockpit. However, the wings were not yet integrated into the vehicle body.

The 1930s was also the era of land-speed records and aerodynamic streamlining. These new shapes, mostly derived from experimentation in the wind tunnel, would soon influence normal car designs, but they played only a minor role in the car market of the day. The purpose of streamlining was to achieve high speeds, but the general public was generally unconvinced of its merits, especially since it inevitably restricted space in the interior. Streamlined design remained essentially an acquisition for motor racing.

A new design era at Mercedes-Benz began in 1932, with the arrival of Hermann Ahrens. Under his auspices, Sindelfingen began to produce exciting and sophisticated vehicles such as the Mercedes-Benz 290, 380, 500K and 770 models.

Mercedes-Benz Type 770, 155/230 HP, 1938.

Type 770 cabriolet.

Type 770 Tourenwagen.

His creative talent broke the mould and added two new aspects to automotive design: sensuality and dynamics. Many of the Ahrens bodies were considered the most spectacular ever created and are still much appreciated by automotive connoisseurs today.

With self-assured style, Mercedes-Benz had successfully brought automotive design to a new level. Today, when experts talk about classic automotive design they immediately refer to the extraordinary dynamic power of the Mercedes-Benz vehicles of this period. Mercedes-Benz did not just equip the exotic models with the new flowing lines and rounded shapes; it also gave them to the 200, 290 and 380 saloons. In spite of the new style, however, Mercedes-Benz vehicles retained their robustness, gaining plaudits for their meticulous attention to detail.

The dream cars of the 1930s were the 500K and 540K models, of which only 761 examples left the production shops from 1935 onwards. With these vehicles, with their voluptuous, flowing lines, Mercedes-Benz had achieved absolute aesthetic perfection, allied with the typical German ideal of a robust and ingenious body. Even today, they are considered objects of perfect beauty.

According to Mercedes-Benz designer Hans-Dieter Futschik, 'The key visual cue of the 540K Roadster is its proportions – the unbelievably long bonnet, the driver's cab set well back just in front of the rear axle, the short tail end. Everything appears to have been stretched out – an aesthetic which remains valid as a design principle today and is still applied to our sports cars.'

In addition, there was the sweep of the wings (a feature that was not exclusive to Mercedes) and the pointed radiator grille, which formed the culminating point of the long tapering engine cowling Already in those days Mercedes vehicles could be identified by their radiator grille, even if other manufacturers copied the shape. A great deal of care was given also to the design of mounted body parts. Gleaming highlights were added in the form of chrome-plated, external exhaust pipes and chrome trim around the wing edges and running the full length of the car. Two spare wheels were mounted at the rear. Viewed as a whole, the ensemble exuded class and aggression.

Unsurprisingly, the sales brochure for the 540 model waxed lyrical about the magic formula behind the new vehicle:

540K special roadster 1936.

540K special coupé 1936.

There cannot be another motor vehicle that is so sur-rounded by the charm of the unusual as the super-charged Mercedes-Benz 540K. The technological perfection and the wondrous elegance and beauty of its bodies make it a pinnacle of German automotive design. The curve of every line, the elegance of the bonnet, the elongated wings and the wedge-shaped split windscreen all combine to give this car an exceptional dynamic character.

Mercedes-Benz also established new design approaches in the field of motor racing. The famous Silver Arrow of 1938, with the internal designation W154, was the first grand prix racing car to feature a very flat body, thereby experiencing less aerodynamic drag than most of its competitors. The new design was only possible, however, because Mercedes-Benz had come up with a specially designed V12 engine of reduced height.

Together with the 500K and 540K models, the W142 320n Coupé firmly established the Mercedes-Benz coupé tradi-tion in the second half of the 1930s. The elegant and sporty car, its roof lower and shorter than that of the saloon, is considered to be one of the classic beauties of the 1930s. As *Automobil Revue* reported in its November issue of 1937, 'in terms of styling and elegant lines, the external appearance of the car continues the lengthy tradition of genuinely beautiful, noble German cars. It avoids the lapses of taste that are currently swimming across The Pond from America.'

In the event, however, none of these classic beauties was to form the basis of the future of Mercedes-Benz. Instead, this honour went to the Mercedes-Benz 170V, which first appeared in 1936. Designed as a model for mass production, it was predestined for styling and design that did away with effects. With its innovative sloping radiator, the body appeared more spacious, sober and functional and yet it still had the charisma and status that might be expected of a Mercedes — and, indeed, is still expected today. In addition, it was clear from the outset that the stylists had aimed for a look that would not require revision for some time and would retain a contemporary feel for many years to come.

540K special **LWB** tourer.

1936 170V saloon.

1936 170V cabriolet.

This objective, termed 'long-life quality', has been high on the list of priorities for Mercedes-Benz designers ever since.

The sales brochure for the 170V promised 'functional beauty – a line that does not seek to be modern by force, but which underscores the car's performance and characteristics: its speed, safe road-holding ability, and the comfort it affords passengers'. However, the Mercedes-Benz 170V had not quite reached the future yet. Although production started up again after the Second World War and continued until 1955, by this time other approaches were being followed, which presented automotive design with a completely new range of stimuli and possibilities.

Design professor Othmar Wickenheiser put the essence of this upheaval in a nutshell: 'In 1946 the Kaiser Frazer heralded the advent of the three-box body era in the USA. The style-giving design features were a continuous shoulder line and complete integration of the wings into the body as a whole.'

That was what the future had in store.

1950–1960: DIFFERENT ROUTES FOR THE USA AND EUROPE

Although times were hard in Europe in the aftermath of the Second World War, economic conditions did begin to improve slowly. Traffic jams were still a rarity on Germany's autobahns, the petrol stations offered nothing but petrol, cars were mostly still bolted together by hand and parking meters had just been introduced.

To a large extent, automotive design in Europe and the USA went down different routes. Europe had been brought to its knees economically by the war and its mobility needs were therefore focused on cheap small cars. Appearance, at least for the time being, was of secondary importance. In the USA, on the other hand, the car was a status symbol and drivers revelled in the excesses of dream car designs. They lusted after panoramic windscreens, fintails and aggressive radiator grilles, while individual components, such as bumper horns, wing tips and even wheel trims, were accorded

1951 170 limousine.

**1952 220 limousine
showing the headlamps,
which were now set
into the wings.**

special styling and emphasis – preferably involving lots of chrome-plating.

New design principles in car making meant that the days of independent bodybuilders were at an end. One reason for this was the introduction of the self-supporting body – a design approach that no longer required a chassis in the 'old' sense of the term. Those parts that would previously have been mounted on the frame were now attached to the body directly.

At Mercedes-Benz, too, a new era was under way. Although various successor versions of the 170 model were built until 1955, the abandonment of pre-war design had begun as early as 1951 – if only cautiously to begin with. It was the 220 model that really set things in motion. Basically, it was a six-cylinder version of the 170S, although the designers had restyled its front wings and integrated the headlamps into them; before, they had been squashed between the wings and the radiator grille. With the headlamps mounted further apart, the 220 suddenly had a much more modern countenance.

Also introduced in 1951 was the Mercedes 300 model, colloquially known as the '300er' or simply the 'Adenauer', since it was the vehicle of choice of the first Chancellor of the new Federal Republic of Germany. The 'Adenauer' clearly demonstrated the transition from the classic shape with freestanding wings and headlamps to the self-supporting chassis-body structure (the 'pontoon' or Ponton design). The headlamps were set wide apart and integrated into the wings, and the momentum from the wings continued deep into the front doors. The rounded wings also helped to compensate visually for the rather bulky front end and oversized volumes.

In 1951, the Mercedes-Benz 300 was the largest and fastest series-produced car made in Germany. The design was a mixture of traditional pre-war shapes and the modern 'pontoon' shape.

The X-oval tube frame of a Type 300 (W186 II), the basic dimensions of which go back to the Type 230 (W153) from before the Second World War.

Another member of the 300 family was the 300 S Coupé, which was based on the shortened 300 chassis. This car continued the Mercedes-Benz coupé tradition, with front and rear wings that retained an individual profile. It was one of the last cars to be built in this way and, as such, was considered to be an elegant farewell to traditional automotive design. According to Werner Breitschwerdt, who later took over as head of body development at Sindelfingen and would eventually become chairman of the board of management of Mercedes-Benz, this coupé was 'by some distance the most beautiful car of its era'.

However, the days of frame construction were numbered; the future of Mercedes-Benz – and all other car manufacturers – lay in the self-supporting body. In the USA, the Ponton design had been introduced in 1946, and eventually all modern cars would feature the smooth-surfaced, simplified body form, stripped of running boards, separately mounted headlamps and protruding wings. From now on, everything would now be integrated into the body.

Europe was a little way behind the USA in adopting the new design and the first European vehicles of this type were not seen until 1950. Mercedes-Benz surprised the automotive world in 1953 with the new 180 model – the first Mercedes-Benz vehicle to adopt the new style. Featuring continuous side walls without freestanding wings, it broke with the styling of the 1930s. Mercedes had completely integrated the wings into the basic body, which also accommodated the engine and luggage compartment in the rear. Out of this arose a harmonious and generously proportioned (by the standards of the day) glazed passenger compartment.

With the Ponton Mercedes, as the vehicle quickly became known colloquially, Mercedes said farewell to the aesthetic ideal of German pre-war cars. The rectangular outline of the new 180 offered distinct advantages, including a more spacious interior, as well as vastly improved aerodynamics combined with much reduced wind noise, thanks to the sleek, solid front end. Compared with the 170S, the interior had grown by 22 per cent, the luggage compartment by an astonishing 75 per cent and the window area of the body by 40 per cent. It was these figures that immediately attracted the attention of potential customers.

The new Ponton design, with its continuous side walls, was popular for technological reasons, too. The self-supporting body, which in the 180 was also supported by a frame-floor assembly, made the vehicle lighter and more torsionally rigid than its predecessor models, immediately improving both agility and handling.

The new shape did not meet with universal approval, however. The Ponton Mercedes represented such a significant break from the styling of its predecessors that it was

1953 Type 180: this would be the last time the Mercedes was not self-supporting.

a major risk for Daimler-Benz. In keeping with its tradition, the company managed to soften the impact by introducing the innovation in parallel with a number of evolved design elements, rather than simply adopting the radically new approach on its own. The Mercedes-Benz 180 continued to feature a noticeably lower bonnet and the circular head-lamps were set into the dynamically sculpted front wings. The elegant rear end fell away gently towards the tail, revealing in the rear wings a masterful momentum reminiscent of the dynamic lines of pre-war automobiles. (This same – often imitated – typical Mercedes design element also reappears in the modern E-Class. The 'sway of the hips' today

The new, modern face of Mercedes-Benz passenger cars after the Second World War was represented by the 180 (1953).

1954 300 SL coupé (gullwing).

The 300 SL coupé showing the gullwing door in the raised position.

The 300 SL coupé space-frame design.

represents solidity and power.) The 180 also featured the typical Mercedes radiator grille, of course, canted steeply into the oncoming wind.

Another product of the 1950s was the legendary 300 SL, whose aura continues to shine even today. Considered the beating heart of the Mercedes sports car legend, it is without doubt one of the most exciting cars ever built. When the 300 SL appeared in 1954, there was something almost revolutionary about it. Combining elegance with the boldness of design that was perceived as condensed aesthetics, for most it remains the ultimate in automotive design of its day.

The 300 SL owed its unusual proportions to a vehicle designed for the racetrack – where it enjoyed many successful outings – by the ingenious Rudolf Uhlenhaut. Friedrich Geiger transformed this racing sports car into the automotive masterpiece that the 300 SL subsequently became. The transformation was not without problems, however. The famous upswept doors gave rise to the 300 SL's affection-

300 SL roadster, sporting the stack headlamps.

ate 'Gullwing' nickname, but they had not been planned as a mere design gimmick. On the contrary, Friedrich Geiger had been forced to accept that conventional doors would be impossible, on account of the car's lightweight tubular racing chassis, which in the interests of rigidity had had to be built up high at the sides. Gullwing doors were therefore the only practical solution.

Geiger then tailored a streamlined body with a sloping and rounded rear end to fit the intricate space-frame chassis, with the wings bulging from it like muscles. In order to accommodate the engine into this precisely crafted body, he positioned impressive power domes on the bonnet. These remain brand-typical elements of current Mercedes-Benz sports cars. The same is true for the lateral cool air vents, designed like gills, and the sickle-shaped 'eyebrows' above the wheel housings, officially known as 'spray guards', as they served to protect the sides of the body from dirt and stones. He also gave the 300 SL a new, broader face, with the Mercedes star at its centre. This face has adorned Mercedes-Benz sports vehicles and coupés ever since.

According to Bruno Sacco, the 300 SL Coupé ranked as one of the most important icons in automotive design: 'There are few vehicles in sports car history that so suc-

The 300 SL frame being carried by workers at Sindelfingen.

cessfully combine performance and superiority with such harmonious yet powerful lines.'

The subsequent roadster model also bore Friedrich Geiger's imprint. Apart from the gullwing doors, the main differences from the coupé were its vertical headlamps. And the 'small' 190 SL, aimed at less affluent customers, borrowed many of the fascinating design details of the 300 SL.

Mercedes designer Hans-Dieter Futschik provided the following analysis of the 300 SL and its design history:

Although probably never intended as such, the 300 SL offers a number of dynamic visual cues that make it almost irresistible. There is something almost human about its figure – a very muscular body, strong shoulders and a broad, athletic back. The glazed area appears small, making the basic body with its short, tight rear and elongated bonnet seem even more athletic. The large wheels create the impression of long legs. In the sum of its parts, the 300 SL exudes pure eroticism. Although design details such as the

eyebrows along the sides, the power domes and the gullwing doors were clearly forced measures, their presence still has a trademark effect even today. Nevertheless, the developers of the day certainly did not set out to design an icon; as the 'forced measures' demonstrate, they set about their task with pragmatism.

In 1954 Mercedes-Benz returned to the elite discipline in motorsport and also broke surprising new stylistic ground in racing car design. In those days, the international grand prix races admitted other body forms, so for fast circuits such as Monza teams developed fully enclosed streamlined models. One such model was the W196, which caused a sensation. Not only was it fast, it was also exceptionally beautiful. After the extremely long, broad, flat bonnet came the centrally positioned cockpit, behind which an air scoop fell gently away to the rear. This scoop picked up the rhythmical momentum of the long, dynamic wings. The flowing lines were broken only by two aerodynamically designed

The 1954 W196 Grand Prix race car (front view).

The W196 Grand Prix car, showing the plan profile with rear air scoop.

rear-view mirrors positioned alongside the dome of the cockpit, to which was fastened a miniscule windscreen. The Mercedes-Benz streamlined grand prix car was like a product of nature, a pebble that had been polished by the flow of water. Function, sensuality and aesthetics came together in a joyous symbiosis.

THE TRANSITION FROM STYLING TO DESIGN

Meanwhile, another style change had been gathering pace abroad. Design Professor Othmar Wickenheiser describes how it happened:

> *The fintail era began overseas in the 1950s. This was a self-conscious reaction to the inflated Ponton volumes, in which body surfaces were smoothed, tautened and equipped in places with contrasting convex-concave surfaces and decorated with distinctive modernist fin shapes at the rear.*

The fintail Mercedes in the design studio.

RIGHT: **Mercedes insisted they had not merely succumbed to trends, but that the fintails were 'guide fins' for reversing.**

Side view of the 220 S WIII (six-cylinder version).

According to many experts, this was the point at which automotive designers finally made the transition from styling to design. Mercedes-Benz was not immune to the changes. In 1959, the company introduced the six-cylinder 220, 220 S and 220 SE saloons of the premium class, which featured moderate yet distinctively transatlantic street-cruising style elements that governed the lines – otherwise known as 'fintails'. In these Mercedes-Benz models, how-ever, they were not bombastic decoration, but moderate and angular. As such, they highlighted the trapezoidal line of the new models to great visual effect. Keen to ensure that the fintails would not be considered mere fashion accesso-ries, Mercedes-Benz in its inimitable way insisted on calling them 'guide fins'. In fact, they did serve a genuinely useful function in parking manoeuvres.

These visual style elements were highly controversial and

Bruno Sacco was forced to make a statement about them in an internal memo:

> *We believe that the design of the rear is not necessarily a North American feature, rather it is a product of the age, for tail wings have regularly been used by Italian body designers since the mid-1950s in connection with aerodynamic studies. If one imagines the car without the proposed tail wings, then in terms of the arrangement of design elements such as lights, bumpers etc., the rear aspect of the 220 SE of 1959 represents the tail configuration that is the most copied and remodelled by other manufacturers of all time.'*

In general, the new prestige class saloon from Mercedes-Benz had clean stylistic lines and did away with superficial elements. The straight lines fell away slightly towards the rear, a lateral edge divided up the large side areas, and a panoramic windscreen and broad sweeping rear window gave a new airy aspect to the glazing. The bonnet was contoured as before and the radiator grille adopted a more or less vertical position as usual, flanked by vertically arranged headlamps – a first for a mass-produced car. The vertical headlamps had previously made their debut in the 300 SL Roadster.

The designers also showed courage in the interior. They installed in the new saloon a vertical speedometer with a vertically rotating column and speed ranges marked in different colours. This design was quickly abandoned, however. On the other hand, there was another innovation that quickly found acceptance and is now a permanent feature in all modern vehicles. This was the steering wheel that was equipped with a padded impact plate at its centre.

Two years later, Mercedes-Benz followed up these saloons with four-cylinder models, which from the windscreen rearwards were identical to the larger models. There were only two differences: the front had been shortened, by 14.5cm, and the new 190 had circular rather than rectangular vertical headlamps.

The fintail model was also significant in that it was the first vehicle to feature a rigid passenger cell and crumple zones. As such, it started a whole new chapter in 'integrated design' – the history of designed-in safety. The era of the fintail Mercedes models also heralded significant changes to the positioning of design within Daimler-Benz. In 1960, the head of the body-testing department was appointed head of passenger car design. With that, the design department became independent.

In spite of America's predilection for dream cars with giant fins and shark heads, the much more formal and restrained premium-class cars from Mercedes-Benz enjoyed great success in the USA. In 1958 almost 14 per cent of all production was sold in the USA, and by 1959 that figure had risen to around 22 per cent. Style, elegance and status had won the day.

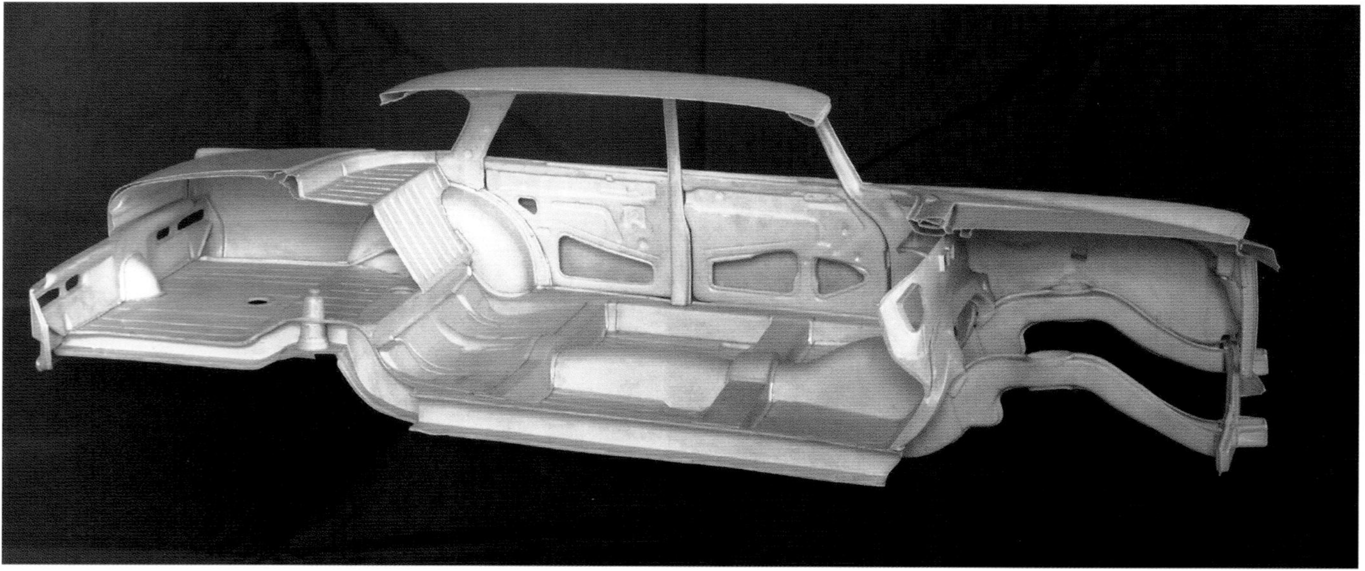

The W111 clearly showing its fine monocoque body in white.

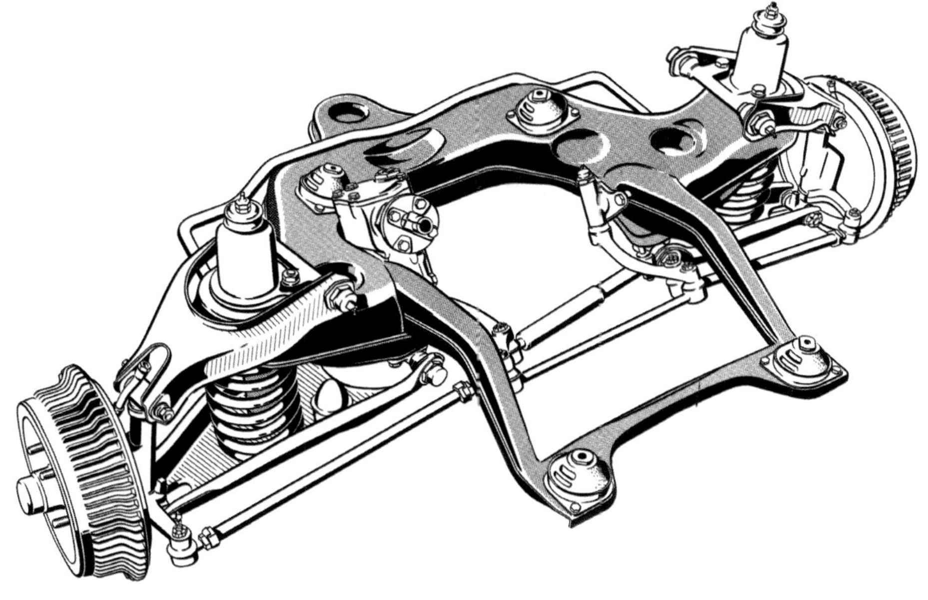

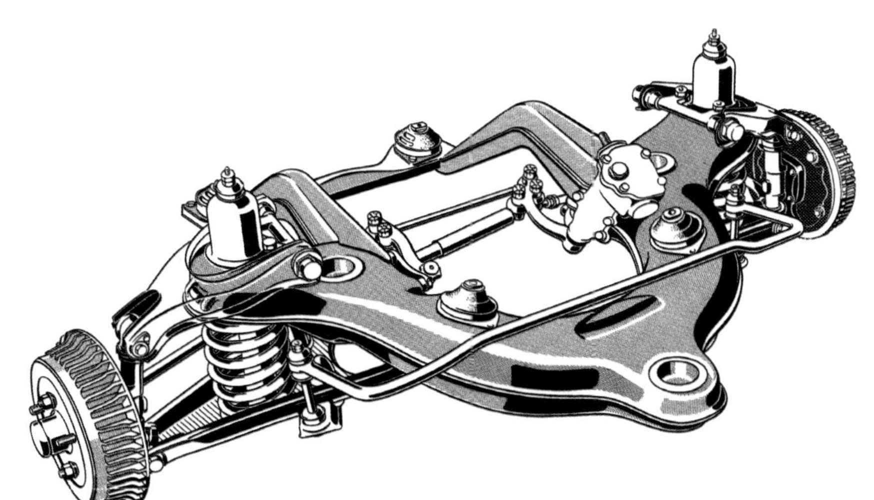

Three box safety zones, as detailed by Béla Barényi.

1960–1975: 'FLOWER POWER' AND MASS MOTORIZATION

Creating a Design Idiom

The 1960s began with great promise. The economy was flourishing on both sides of the Atlantic and the boom times were back. Prosperity returned and people had more money to spend on cars. Intermediate class vehicles in particular achieved record sales in Europe.

Once Mercedes-Benz discovered its own design idiom, many of its vehicles became exciting and eye-catching, while at the same time clearly reflecting the basic values of the brand: quality, reliability, innovation and emotion. The company quickly learned however that successful design is based not just around the object but also around the end user, and his or her needs and expectations. It has to take into account the physical and intellectual aspects of those needs, as well as emotions and beliefs. This is where automotive design differs from art. Good design does have to appeal to the senses and offer new perspectives, but good automotive design also has to evolve continually, creating a product that appears fresh and new.

In the 1960s, designers were having to consider economic, environmental, ecological, safety and social aspects for the first time. By the middle of the decade, cars with American design features had disappeared almost entirely from the model ranges of European manufacturers, and from the period onwards, motor vehicle design trends were set in Europe. Trapezoidal bodies with straight lines and large glazed areas became state-of-the-art – in growing traffic density and for parking, this set-up ensured good visibility. Despite this new age of reason, however, chrome trim was still ubiquitous for window frames, exterior mirrors and bumpers.

Then, in the early 1970s, as a global oil crisis loomed, the car began to lose its innocence. Sunday driving bans in Germany in 1973 meant it was impossible to ignore the signs that motoring had to change. Aerodynamics engineers forced a rethink in the design departments at automotive manufacturers, and even more intensive use was made of the wind tunnel. The quest for lower aerodynamic drag was reflected in body designs, and became visible even to the layman. Streamlined trim was introduced, to integrate bumpers and side mirrors into the design of the body. Body shapes became smoother and wedge-shaped, with a flat bonnet offering less resistance to the oncoming airflow. Development of the aerodynamic wedge shape was a pioneering step that was to influence automotive design for years to come.

Protestors have an Autobahn sit-in on car-free Sunday.

An Autobahn barbecue on car-free Sunday.

'Stroke Eight' – A Saloon with Cult Status

In 1968, Mercedes-Benz introduced the W115/114 series as the successor to the 'small fintail' and as a new, elegant definition of the intermediate class. Given the internal designation '/8', to denote the year of its birth, the vehicle family quickly acquired the affectionate nickname 'Stroke Eight'. And it proved itself to be a true child of 1968, not only at the cutting edge both technically and stylistically, but also slightly revolutionary.

With this vehicle, Mercedes-Benz bade farewell to the cross-series concept of the three-box body, which had been

The first new-generation model range W114 'Stroke Eight'.

The W114's classic lines, with the 'Mercedes touch', ensured it would always look like a Mercedes.

The first W114 off the line at Sindelfingen.

Even as a taxi, the W114 would turn heads with its elegant understated lines.

used since the war for Ponton and fintail designs in particular. The key features of this first independent body form for the intermediate series had been established by chief engineer Fritz Nallinger as early as 1960. Instead of following fashion, he wanted to rigorously embrace the ideal of simple elegance and clean lines. With a classically modern silhouette, without superfluous detail, the saloon exuded not only solidity and a love of detail and technical invention, but also a freshness and sportiness. While it was considered by some to have an Italian-style nimbleness, its Mercedes origins would also be immediately recognizable – even if there were no star on the bonnet.

Over its nine-year production period, the Stroke Eight became a cultural automotive icon of the time. Marking its 35th birthday, Spiegel Online wrote: 'The intermediate class saloon of 1968–1976 is a paragon of automotive objectivity – and yet it achieved genuine cult status.'

Mercedes designer Hans-Dieter Futschik gives the following contemporary assessment of the saloon of 68:

The Stroke 8 is very linear, two-dimensional and sensible in design. Even the front end, with its boxy

headlamps, was made more objective. But there was no attempt to abandon chrome. The headlamps are framed in chrome, and the seam marking the top edge of the side wall is also characterized by chrome trim. This trim also has a practical purpose as a protective rub strip. For this same reason, the bumper is equipped with a rubber strip. In general, however, the vehicle has a thoroughly baroque feel.

CIII – Ahead of Its Time

The CIII sports car was another sensational car that was developed during the era of Friedrich Geiger. Owing its shape to the future head of design, Bruno Sacco, the CIII had the impact of an entirely new breed of highly trained athlete. It had initially been conceived as a test vehicle for the development of Wankel's engine technology, but it became ingrained in the memory essentially for its striking and hugely exciting design.

For the designated test vehicle, the designers under Bruno Sacco's aegis were given complete freedom to aban-

The CIII, designed by Bruno Sacco, blew the boxy 1960s styles out of the water.

The C111 was never meant for production.

don traditional design approaches. They developed a vehicle that was highly original, independent and radically different from production vehicles bearing the three-pointed star at the time. It also contained a wealth of details that would later be used in other Mercedes-Benz vehicles as well as by other vehicle brands.

While most cars on the road during the 1960s and 70s were box-shaped designs that paid little attention to aerodynamics, the C111 was trimmed to be as streamlined as possible. Numerous world-speed records stood as testimony to the aerodynamic effectiveness of its revolutionary design. An extreme wedge shape and upward swinging gullwing doors stood apart from the automotive masses, high-quality sports cars included. The unusual interplay of surfaces and edges coined a new style that would later be frequently copied.

It should be noted also that the C111 lacked the distinctive Mercedes face. It never went into series production, even though Untertürkheim received numerous orders, many of them accompanied by blank cheques.

Pagoda – An Exciting Roofline

In 1963, when Mercedes-Benz discontinued production of the 300 SL and 190 SL, the all-in-one successor was an SL model that created a sensation, above all for its unusual exterior. The new head-turner from Stuttgart was the 230 SL, which boasted a quite iconoclastic appearance that differed from all other cars in terms of its unusual proportions and lines. Its dominant design feature – which many observers initially found disturbing – was a removable coupé roof that broke every previous mould by sloping towards the centre of the vehicle. Utterly unique and reminiscent of Japanese temple architecture, this SL quickly became known colloquially as the 'Pagoda'.

With its Pagoda roof, the 230 SL was further proof that the designers at Mercedes-Benz were continually seeking ingenious ways to combine core brand values, such as quality, solidity and stylish, self-confident elegance, with bold and innovative elements. The results were not only lasting design milestones, but also brought a breath of fresh air to automotive design. Then, as now, the Mercedes-Benz design philosophy was about retaining what was tried and tested,

The **W113 SL** was known as the 'Pagoda' due to its curved roofline.

The rear of the **W113** clearly shows the curve of the roofline.

Béla Barényi and Paul Bracq demonstrating the strength of the Pagoda roof by fitting it to an experimental W111.

while at the same time setting new trends. Then, as now, however, the designers were not interested in creating art for art's sake. Often revolutionary design ideas concealed deliberations that were based on very practical considerations.

The Pagoda roof of the 230 SL was a case in point. Its development was based above all on safety considerations. Mercedes engineer Béla Barényi, the pioneer of modern passenger-car safety technology, had designed and patented this unconventional roof form in 1956, because it had the capacity to withstand extreme loads and thus offered vehicle occupants optimum safety in the event of an accident. Similarly impressive was the degree of headroom offered by the 230 SL when the Pagoda roof was in place.

Mercedes designer Hans-Dieter Futschik wrote of the 230 SL: 'The Pagoda is unbelievably slim and elongated; with little panelling above the wheel and a low waistline, it is as if one were sitting in the open air. The entire vehicle has a horizontal orientation. Like many of the cars of the 1960s, it is very linear and not at all overloaded.'

Auto, motor und sport remarked on the Pagoda's 'unusual, almost provocative shape. These lines really demand discussion: a sports car should always be a feast for the eyes – indeed many people pay for the looks alone.'

Stirling Moss – arguably the best driver of his day, and one who piloted Mercedes-Benz racing sports cars to many international victories – also confessed to being an admirer of the 230 SL. In a letter dated 20 March 1964 to Alfred Neubauer, who forwarded a copy to Fritz Nallinger, the British driver was full of praise for the car:

> *I can't remember in all my years of driving ever having driven a car (racing cars excluded!) that I would more have liked to own.*
>
> *I'm excited by this car, let me briefly explain why. The equipment, for a start – as ever with Mercedes, one sees the quality. The entirely new lines are functional yet very elegant. The most striking change from the conventional Mercedes silhouette is the revolutionary roofline; it is slightly concave – and this basically simple innovation gives the car an extraordinarily sporty appearance. But it is not just the exterior that benefits; so, too, does the outstanding visibility in the coupé's interior. The high windows and narrow window pillars guarantee almost complete all-round visibility. Whether as a sporty saloon with hard top*

or a racy convertible with fully retractable soft top – the 230 SL looks good. There is no other word for it. No superfluous chrome, the overall impression is solid – and elegant.

Mercedes-Benz 600 – The State Car

In September 1963, Mercedes-Benz launched a true heavyweight on to the world stage – the 600 model, which is still celebrated today. This saloon offered a new definition of exclusive representational vehicles. Designed to be the ultimate in sophistication, it was technologically state-of-the-art.

The ultimate Mercedes: the W100 600.

The 600 was named 'the world's finest car' many times over.

The appearance alone of this frequently used state limousine was impressive. On a 3200mm wheelbase, the Mercedes stylists had built a modern yet majestic body of opulent spaciousness. The ensemble was dominated by straight, unfussy lines, elongated flanks and generous glazed areas. Long, vertical headlamps left plenty of space for the mighty radiator grille, making it appear even more distinctive than the customary Mercedes radiator design. Broad chrome trim framed not only the windows but also the wheel housings, with the radiator and door handles also decorated with gleaming chrome. In spite of the objective sobriety of the basic body of the Mercedes-Benz 600, the saloon exuded power and solidity.

The trade press did not hold back in its praise for the 600. *Car and Driver* called it simply 'the world's finest car', while the British trade magazine *The Autocar* considered it to be 'the world's greatest sports car'.

The SL-Class

One of the absolute Mercedes-Benz classics was the SL-Class, introduced in 1971 with the internal designation R107. The first models came off the production line just as the first lunar vehicle set off across the surface of the Moon; the last example coincided with Mikhail Gorbachev's declaration of *Glasnost* in the USSR. Eighteen years had passed. America had seen five US Presidents come and go, while Germany had had three Chancellors.

The fact that this SL generation enjoyed the favour of customers for so long was due in no small measure to its dynamic, timeless appearance. Racing driver Hans Her-

Early Geiger designs of what the R107 might be.

rmann described it thus: 'It is powerful and yet no muscle man. There is something supremely efficient about it, something masculine.'

The body of the R107 presented the observer with comprehensive curves and opulent chrome work. In some circles the newcomer was even referred to as a 'neo-baroque creation'. In fact, the lines of this SL family had been drawn with great care and finesse. For example, the boot lid picked up the design of the concave roofline, to achieve a harmonious overall image. However, the designers of the SL consciously avoided stylistic escapades. It was as if they had guessed that, by giving it uncomplicated lines, they were equipping it with the source of its longevity. Stylistic innovations included the first horizontal headlamps and wraparound indicators.

The R107 actually became something of an automotive monument, its übercool 1970s charm making it virtually ageless. It was as if the details had been carved off the same block and had been crafted for eternity. And no wonder: the Mercedes engineers had set themselves the goal of giving an open-top vehicle the stability of a saloon.

However, the technology was anything but archaic. In keeping with SL tradition, the R107 was highly innovative, as demonstrated by numerous small but creative ideas. For example, it was the first car to feature distinctive horizontal cross-ribbing for the tail lamps, to reduce soiling. Such features showed how Mercedes-Benz was applying its expertise in safety to its design, right down to the smallest detail.

The safety concept was completed by further innovative details in the interior. The instrument panel was covered in energy-absorbing PVC foam and the knee area with impact-absorbing upholstery. Another new idea was also the door handle without a door button. Instead the door was opened by pulling on the grip, thereby preventing the door from opening unintentionally in the event of an impact.

The sales brochure described the design of the R107 series as follows:

The front end – known the world over simply as the 'SL radiator' – and the gently rising sideline express the performance readiness of the SL models. The key features include a distinctive, athletic silhouette, which reveals the low centre of gravity is immediately recognizable at a distance and remains untainted by short-term tastes in fashion. The distinctive spoiler in the lower part of the front apron makes active handling even safer, thanks to reduced lift at the front axle. Protective trim at the flanks reduce soiling of the upper body areas.

PROJECT X: THE 'GULLWING REPLACEMENT'?

On 11 June 1955 at Le Mans, a Mercedes-Benz W196 S racer was catapulted into the crowd, resulting in the death of 88 spectators. The tragic events changed everything at Daimler-Benz. Its substantial (and virtually unbeatable) racing programme was cancelled at the end of that year, and there was clearly an effect on its road-car product planning from that moment. There was no real standalone sports car for the brand, to replace the highly desirable Gullwing from previous decades. This is probably one of the reasons why the W113 was relatively tame in comparison with its predecessor, the W198

The ripple effect following the accident was felt almost immediately at Daimler, with the company embarking on a period of intensive research into improving secondary safety – protecting the occupants of cars involved in accidents. First, there was an internal shake-up. Having previously headed the experiment and research department, Karl Wilfert was asked to manage a new amalgamated 'stylist department', bringing together Fritz Nallinger, Hans Scherenberg, Friedrich Geiger and Béla Barényi.

Wilfert's influence had been especially evident in the

(continued overleaf...)

In this sketch dated May 1962, although the overall W113 shape has been retained, it is clearly longer from front wheel to firewall and has hints of the W198-style air vent.

More hints at the Pagoda W113.

(continued from previous page)

designs of the SL sport-cars, first the 300 SL Gullwing and more recently the Pagoda-topped W113. In the early 1960s, he initiated a project for a car that was purported to be the spiritual successor to the Gullwing W198. This car was referred to later on by Daimler-Benz as the 'SLX', however in reality the programme does not seem to have had an official name or designation, although there were a number of code designations, including X, SL X, SL-X, 700 SL, 300 SLX and even C101/111. In one of Giorgio Battistella's sketches there is even a nod to the 230 SL, with a small plaque in the rear parcel shelf clearly denoting '230 Coupé'.

These undated images may represent the next phase – the top rendering has a split headlamp level similar to that of the W113 sketches. Both shapes feature the elongated footprint of the 300 SLX sketch and the Pagoda roof, although the C-post was much finer on the top example. The bottom rendering has a fared

nostril face similar to that used by Paul Bracq in his 1958 exploratory sketch for a 6.3 sportster.

Not only does the above image bear no similarity to the W113, it also hints at the later C111 shape. The lengthened roofline seems to have been influenced by the Ferrari 250 GTO or even the Volvo P1800, which also later went on to be offered as a 'shooting brake' version called the P1800ES late in the early 1970s. The 'shooting brake' concept was certainly in vogue at this time. The gullwing doors make their first reappearance here, as does the suggestion of a rear-/mid-engined configuration. It was also known that a Porsche 904 had been purchased by Daimler-Benz to evaluate the concept further.

The shaping shows a clear distinction from that of the W113, bringing in much more curvature and tighter form detailing; this was down to the unusual recruitment of Giorgio Battistella, who was placed under Paul Bracq as a stylist in 1964. From the first day, these three creative

The 600 sportster rendering was perhaps just free thinking.

This sketch shows where the SLX look was going, as it took on a completely new configuration.

The influence of the 904 (top) is most obvious from the Bracq rendering, but overall the styling language had changed.

minds – Bracq, Bruno Sacco and Battistella – would work together for many long hours, with many long discussions and many sketches, to consider a car that would abandon all the rules that had applied up until that time. Paul Bracq, who had the last word as chief designer, finally validated the project of a funny flat car designed by Battistella – but it was never to be. Following the retirement of Fritz Nallinger, and his replacement by Hans Scherenberg, all experimental projects were suspended. When it came to making a decision, Scherenberg voted alongside the board of directors to shelve Project SL-X in favour of something else, the C101.

There are no real details of the progress of the project in the Daimler-Benz archive. They seem to have had so little idea about it that, when they exhibited the wooden model without engine and no interior mock-up in 2010, they referred to it as the 'Sacco Study'. It is possible that, as Sacco had been appointed as development engineer,

working alongside Bracq and Battistella, and had later led the C111 styling effort, Daimler-Benz had confused the two and had retrospectively credited him with the SL-X.

Both Paul Bracq and Giorgio Battistella left the employ of Daimler-Benz shortly after. Bruno Sacco was devastated at the withdrawal of the project and always regretted that it never came to fruition, as it would have been a true replacement to the 300 SL Gullwing.

While the SL-X project was shelved, a small team made up of engineers and designers was assigned to work on a new sports car known as the C101 as early as 1967, according to the archives. Officially, Daimler made it known that it had never asked the group to build a successor to the 300 SL Gullwing or specifically to the 113 SL; the car it was working on had never been intended to see the inside of a showroom. Instead, it was a rolling laboratory that could be used to test out new features and ideas.

Giorgio Battistella (left) and Paul Bracq (right).

The wooden SL-X model is now on display at the Mercedes-Benz museum in Untertürkheim.

A 2+2 version similar to the final model version, although room for a rear or mid-engine was very unlikely.

Rear view of the wooden SL-X model.

CHAPTER TWO

DESIGNING THROUGH SAFETY AND ACCIDENT RESEARCH

THE 1930S: FIRST VEHICLE TESTS

Mercedes-Benz engineers first began to take a closer look at what 'vehicle accident safety' really meant in the early 1930s, more than twenty years before the first crash test was performed. However, they were not conducting research into passive safety, but what became known as 'active safety' — that is to say, the way a vehicle behaves mechanically. The aim initially was to eliminate annoying vibrations caused by the engine and drivetrain.

LATE 1930S TO LATE 1940S

The year 1939 was a key date in the safety history of Daimler-Benz, with the recruitment of engineer Béla Barényi, whose developments were destined to become benchmarks for passive safety in modern passenger cars. More than 2,500 of Barényi's inventions were patented, included the safety body with a rigid passenger cell and front and rear crumple zones (premiered in 1959 in the W111 series), and the safety steering wheel, which made its debut in 1976 in the 123 model series.

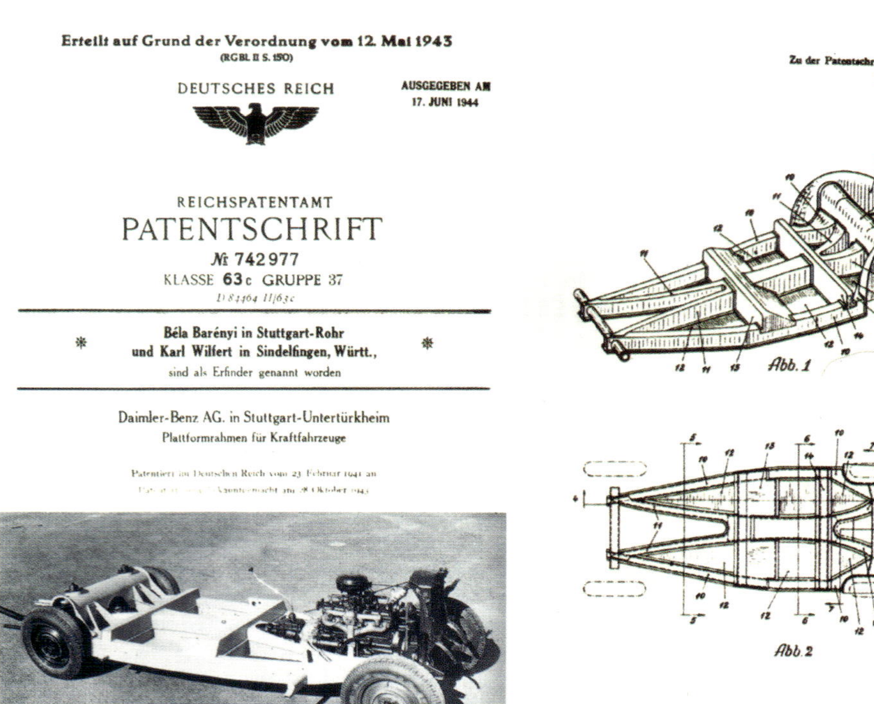

In the early 1940s various experimental chassis were built for safety tests. This is car 11, a platform framework very close to what was used later on the 170V.

THE 1950S

At the time when Barényi and his colleagues were bringing the safety body to production standard in the 1950s, the prevailing view was still that the interests of occupant safety were best served by maximum rigidity in the body. Later crash tests showed, however, that, although rigid body structures performed well in accidents, they passed on most of the kinetic energy generated to the occupants, which often resulted in serious injury.

The Barényi safety body, patented in 1951, represented a major advance in terms of passive safety. Featuring crumple zones that would deform in a controlled way, it offered for the first time a way of substantially reducing the kinetic energy that reached occupants in the event of an accident. It had been developed as the result of careful observation, technical imagination and a readiness to engage in visionary thinking.

As well as the body structure, many other aspects of the passenger car were improved and revised in terms of safety during this period. These included details such as door locks, interior upholstery and padding, windscreens made from safety glass and seat belts.

During the 1950s, the Daimler-Benz engineers watched closely as crash testing established itself in the USA as a new instrument for research and development. Visits to US universities and automobile manufacturers provided the experts from Stuttgart with inspiration and ideas for their own component testing and crash tests. On one such visit, in 1955, to the Ford crash-testing facility in Dearborn, Karl Wilfert, Rudolf Uhlenhaut and Fritz Nallinger were surprised to discover that Ford was already using accident research for aggressive marketing purposes. Not long after, this would influence the way Mercedes-Benz dealt with the sensitive issue of vehicle safety.

The W111 series benefited from the first vehicle safety tests conducted by the engineers at Stuttgart. Although there were no crash tests as yet, in the precise sense of the term, since 1956 and 1957 the company's own researchers had been testing individual vehicle components to study how they behaved in accidents. The introduction of these tests represented a major watershed in safety research at

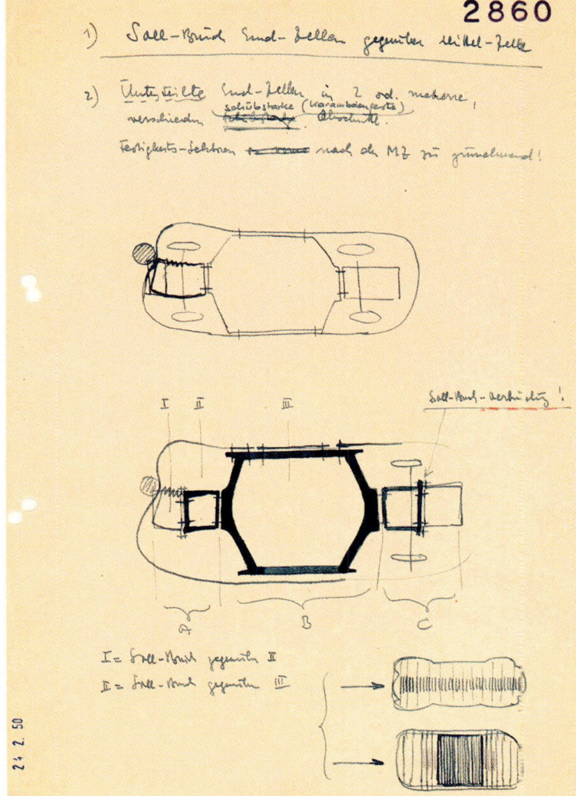

Crumple zone testing.

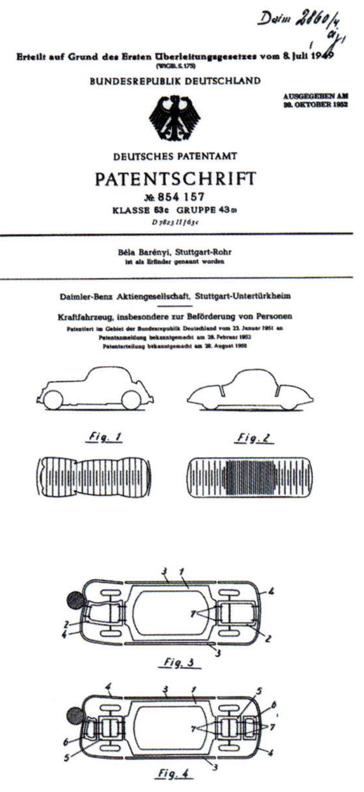

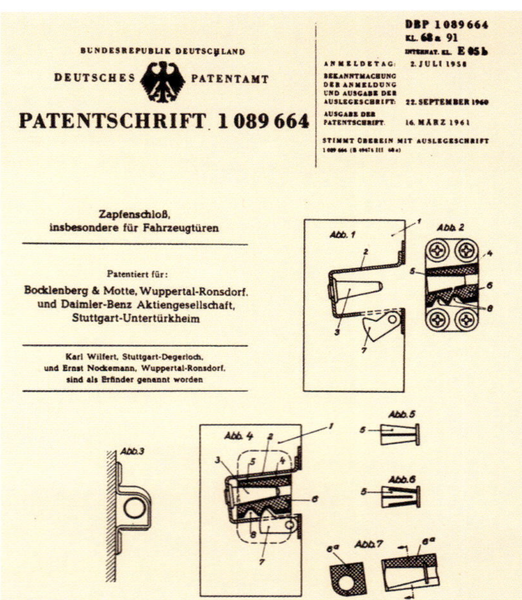

Béla Barényi safety lock.

Testing the W111 to destruction, something Mercedes would continue to do with every model.

Testing interiors (passive safety) with test dummies.

Mercedes-Benz. Until then, the only information on passive vehicle safety had come from assessments of crashed vehicle. A few years earlier, the glazing industry had developed a simulator to study the behaviour of safety glass, and had used this to analyse the impact of a human head against a front windscreen. Mercedes-Benz used similar apparatus to test the padded surface of instrument panels: a spring fired a 5-kg wooden ball at the component being tested, while a tracer registered the deceleration of the artificial head striking the padding. Step by step, the engineers used the dummy head to test other components in the vehicle interior.

The impact tests demonstrated the inherent danger not only of protruding components, but also of wooden trim, which had a tendency to splinter. Many customers, particularly those who bought luxury models, preferred genuine wood as a material for interior fittings, so Mercedes-Benz developed a multi-layered composite material with aluminium inserts that prevented this splintering effect.

With the development of a new restraint system – the seat belt – in the late 1950s, came the need for a reliable testing procedure. The solution developed in 1959 was the test sled, originally suspended so that it could be swung with acceleration against a fixed object. As well as the seat belt, padded steering wheel impact absorbers and similar components were tested in the accident simulator.

The swinging test sled subsequently gave way to a horizontal test sled on rails, which was accelerated using steel springs. The driver or passenger was represented by a dummy that had been purchased from the USA. This early test dummy, which was also used in the first crash tests, was given the name 'Oscar' by its guardians.

DEVELOPMENTS IN CRASH TESTING

The aim of all the developments from the Mercedes-Benz accident researchers in the late 1950s was to simulate a crash as comprehensively as possible. Accordingly, there was no alternative to the crash test – a procedure that was time-consuming and difficult to control. It was also costly, since it involved subjecting a full vehicle, complete with crash test dummies, to a controlled collision that resulted in corresponding deformation.

At the first Mercedes-Benz crash test, on 10 September 1959, a test car was accelerated head on into a fixed barrier made of old press dies, which otherwise had been destined for the scrap heap. It was the opening of a new chapter in the history of the brand's safety research. The behaviour of vehicles and occupants in car accidents could now be

Early testing dummies for steering wheel safety.

investigated in realistic circumstances. In the decades that followed, Mercedes-Benz continued to set new standards in a line of research that applied throughout the industry. In the process, the company achieved lasting improvements in vehicle safety for the benefit of all road users.

Following the first crash test, the engineers took stock for a while in order to evaluate the new procedure. Crash testing was conducted again on three further test days in March and April 1960. This included the simulation of complete accidents – for example, a side-impact collision between a vehicle from the W111 series and a saloon from the same series. Frontal collisions were carried out once again and rollover tests were introduced for the first time. From the 1960s onwards, the crash test procedure became established as a reliable instrument for optimizing and testing vehicle safety. And at Mercedes-Benz, the detailed crash tests were carried out not just on passenger cars, but also on vans, commercial vehicles and coaches.

Crash testing involved catapults, ramps and concrete walls.

Steam jet-propelled W110.

DEVELOPING THE CRASH TEST DUMMY

In the early years, 'Oscar', the test dummy manufactured by Alderson Research, remained the only one in use in crash testing at Sindelfingen. Later dummies were equipped with load cells for recording acceleration values (these had been in use in the USA since 1952). For the first time, it was possible to have reproducible data on the stresses to which the human body was subjected in a car accident.

The tests conducted by Mercedes-Benz after 1959 led to advances in more areas than just vehicle safety. The dummies were also developed and refined. First of all, new dummies were designed with body proportions corresponding to the average sizes for men, women and children. The precision with which specific test types were conducted was also constantly improved.

In addition to dummy passengers, there was also a test dummy that could be used to simulate accidents involving pedestrians.

Dummies were also developed to measure specific accident scenarios with great precision and, later, highly specialized dummies were used in tests other than crash tests. One example is the climate dummy, which was used to determine the influence of air temperature and humidity on the human body.

'Oscar', the first test dummy, remained a valuable member of the team even after more sophisticated test dummies had been procured. In 1972, the dummy team comprised eight colleagues including 'Oscar', who was deployed for three full decades in the Mercedes-Benz safety research department.

More often than not, front-seat passengers were simulated using sandbags or shop-window mannequins.

Front-end testing with observations by Béla Barényi.

Pioneering tests with older cars made it possible to design a ramp that rotated the test cars about their longitudinal axis in mid-air so that they landed on their roof. This allowed the safety experts to measure the effects on the vehicle body in the event of a rollover accident. Another key element during this second year of crash testing was the company's public relations policy on accident research: Mercedes-Benz invited the press to attend the day of testing on 11 April 1960, where an official presentation of the latest approaches to safety research was given. Clearly, the experts believed that the importance of vehicle safety now outweighed any previously held concerns about mentioning the issue of accidents in customer communications.

The great advantage of crash testing compared with crash vehicle analysis lay in the opportunities the former offered to record the actual events of the crash in every detail. The analytical technology, which had been developed in the years leading up to 1959, included the use of acceleration sensors fitted to the test car, as well as high-speed film that could reproduce images in extreme slow motion.

By the mid-1960s, the first-generation sleds had given way to a new type of impact vehicle, to which a complete car body could be attached for load testing if required. Over the years, crash-test technology was steadily improved. To begin with, a winch was used to accelerate the car, since

this could not be done under the power of its own engine. Borrowing the method used by glider pilots at the Technical University in Stuttgart to launch their aircraft, Mercedes-Benz would launch brand-new saloon cars into the air. The test car would take off from the corkscrew ramp at a speed of 75–80km/h, which would produce the rotation required for the vehicle to roll over in mid-air and land on its roof. The result of these tests was the inclusion of stabilizing elements in the body.

Although it was certainly spectacular, the winch system proved less than ideal, as did the frontal test – sometimes, the test vehicle missed the barrier or stationary car completely. Testing in those days was conducted in the open air at Sindelfingen, and the plant fire service had to be called out more than once to salvage a test car from the Schwippe, the river that ran beside the site.

Ernst Fiala, at that time head of the testing department for passenger car bodies in Sindelfingen, came up with a solution in 1962. He designed a hot-water rocket for the crash tests, which powered the vehicles without the use of a tow line. Fiala received critical advice for his design from the Institute for Jet Propulsion Physics at Stuttgart Airport. Mounted on a single-axle trailer, the apparatus was attached to the rear of the test vehicle and consisted of a pressure tank, a fast-opening valve and a discharge nozzle. To create

Steam jet-powered crash-test apparatus.

thrust, the tank was three-quarters filled with water prior to the experiment and heated until the water temperature reached around 260 degrees centigrade. When the valve was opened, the excess pressure accelerated the car and rocket ensemble to speeds in excess of 100km/h.

The introduction of the hot-water rocket also led to improvements in the test track: reinforced concrete was used for the runway, and the test vehicles and propulsion system were now guided on rails. A fence was also erected to prevent cars landing in the river.

Improvements such as these to the test facilities not only benefited in-house testing. From 1962 to 1967, Mercedes-Benz carried out testing on new types of motorway crash barriers on behalf of the German federal state of Baden-Württemberg. The test strip was also lengthened in 1964 from 65 metres to 90 metres to allow heavier passenger cars to be crash tested, such as the 600 from the W100 series.

MERCEDES-BENZ RESEARCH: A NEW DEPARTMENT

In Germany in the 1960s, accident research was increasingly seen as an issue of national importance. Between 1960 and 1969, more than 157,000 people died on West Germany's roads. One year later, accident statistics reached a record level, with 19,193 fatalities and 531,795 people injured. Research into actual crash events therefore became an indispensable tool in Mercedes-Benz safety development. In May 1969, with the support of the police and the state of Baden-Württemberg, company engineers officially conducted the first systematic analysis and documentation of serious traffic accidents involving Mercedes-Benz passenger cars at the accident site, focusing on the objective impact of the crash on the occupants.

In November 1969, Hans Scherenberg, the regular member of the board of management responsible for development, gave the green light to establish Mercedes-Benz Research. The new department would prove to be the cradle of many important developments in motor vehicle technology, such as the anti-lock braking system (ABS), the airbag and the navigation system. Staff member Hans-Joachim Förster was given responsibility for setting up the department and preparations began immediately. His task was to look at a number of urgent questions that were being asked at the time, including calls for vehicle drive systems with lower emissions and for increasingly safer vehicles. As a qualified engineer, he knew that the company needed to find convincing answers if it was to remain at the forefront of automotive technology and continue to set benchmarks in the industry.

THE FOUR AREAS OF SAFETY

After representatives from Mercedes-Benz had learned about crash tests at Ford in the US in 1955, they also began attending the Stapp car crash conferences. One of the main contributions from Stuttgart in the early years was a presentation by Karl Wilfert (head of the testing department for passenger car bodies in Sindelfingen) entitled 'Comprehensive Vehicle Safety Development', given at the 10th Stapp conference in 1966. It was intended to put an end to the general terminological confusion in categorizing vehicle safety issues. The content is explained in Heike Weishaupt's book on passive safety:

> *Together with Barényi, he made a clear distinction.... During a presentation on vehicle safety to the press, Hans Scherenberg, Member of the Board of Management responsible for Development..., publicly explained this division between the different safety measures. Driving, driver fitness and operating safety were allocated to the area of active safety. Passive safety includes the external and internal safety of the vehicle, which needs to be taken into account as early as the development and design stages.*
>
> *Because of its simplicity and structural preciseness, the distinction proposed by Mercedes-Benz between active and passive safety finally prevailed, with just a few more precise definitions.*

Active Safety
To ensure the maximum level of active safety, the driver needs to be able to predict and control the responses of the vehicle – even when approaching the critical limits of road-holding. Here we shall describe the systems used for axles, steering and brakes, and the assistance systems themselves.

Perceptual Safety
For safety, it is essential firstly that the driver has good visibility, for example with good illumination of the road surface from modern lighting systems, and secondly that the vehi-

**Dr JP Stapp
crash-test sled.**

Dr Stapp accelerated in 5 seconds from a standstill to 632 miles an hour. The sled then decelerated to a dead stop in 1.4 seconds, subjecting Dr Stapp to pressures 40 times the pull of gravity.

cle can be clearly perceived by other road users.

Driver Fitness Safety

Driving a car can be strenuous and tiring. All of the vehicle occupants, for example, have to cope with irritations like vibrations, noises, inadequate air conditioning and uncomfortable seats. The driver has the additional burden of operating the vehicle, particularly on long journeys. This includes accelerating, braking, staying in the correct lane, maintaining distance or driving bumper-to-bumper. If the driver is alert and relaxed, the probability of errors occurring in traffic situations is greatly reduced.

Everything that enhances the vehicle parameters affecting driver fitness safety, for example the spring and damper systems, will thus also enhance driver efficiency.

Functional and Comfort Safety

These include switches that are ergonomically and correctly positioned, and straightforward, intuitive operation of the different vehicle functions. What is meant here are operating concepts that ensure the driver can concentrate on the most important activity, actually driving the vehicle.

The US government issued an invitation to foreign countries to take part in the Enhanced Vehicle Safety Committee (EEVC).

INTERIOR DESIGN

At the end of the 1960s, when Mercedes-Benz first began systematic accident analysis, experts initially focused on improving protection inside the passenger compartment. Although Mercedes models were already fitted with seat belts at that time, very few people actually bothered to use them. For many front-seat passengers, this casual attitude resulted in serious head injuries, from impact with the steering wheel, instrument panel or windscreen. Accident researchers therefore set about identifying dangerous impact points inside the vehicle and suggested improvements to the design of various switches and handles that were responsible for severe injuries. The instrument panel and interior trim materials were also reconsidered with safety in mind. Designers favoured energy-absorbing materials, including a multi-layered composite with aluminium inserts, which could be used where the splintering of wood might be an issue.

Safety measures involved changed interiors, with padded steering wheels and recessed switches.

For safety reasons, any necessary extrusions were rubber formed and wood veneer was backed in aluminium plate.

Förster presented a detailed organization chart straight away, in November 1969. He had very clear ideas about how research by a car manufacturer could produce important findings for the series production of vehicles. The specialist areas in the early days were 'Future–Environment–Transport', 'Vehicle', 'Drive System' and 'Engineering Physics'. The structure of the organization covered virtually all the issues at that time, ranging from low-emissions combustion engines and electric vehicles, infinitely variable transmissions, sensors, assistance systems, body technology, brake technology and headlights, through to mobility in the future.

EARLY 1970S

The Accident Research Centre

By the late 1960s, more and more crash tests were being carried out, with significant importance being attached to the results. The increased activity highlighted the capacity limitations and inadequacies of the old test track in Sindelfingen. The increasingly sophisticated testing technology made it necessary for tests to be carried out regardless of the weather conditions. Accordingly, when construction began in 1972 on a new accident research centre at the Sindelfingen plant, a decision was made to include a 100-metre-long testing hall. The company was one of just a few that would be able to conduct all its crash tests indoors.

The new centre tested and improved restraint systems, seats, steering systems, instrument panels and other safety-related components. Initially, a Bendix sled was installed for crash simulation purposes. In 1972, construction work began on a new crash installation that would also facilitate frontal and side-impact collisions. The engineers opted for a linear motor with a thrust of 53,000 Newtons as a drive system to propel the test vehicle along the 65-metre test track. This power unit accelerated the cars to the target speed over the first half of the track, and then regulated the speed over the remaining distance to the desired value before decoupling in advance of the collision. In one direction of the track, the test cars crashed into a 1000-tonne barrier resting on a sensitive force plate. Rollover tests were conducted in the opposite direction. Collisions involving other vehicles, on the other hand, were still conducted on an open-air site.

The research centre had the very latest and most efficient installations to simulate crashes, providing excellent

The original sled test rig.

THE OFFSET CRASH TEST

From the early 1970s, Mercedes-Benz was a pioneer in the field of accident research with its crash analyses. Information was collected on the type and exact sequence of crashes, the deformation behaviour of vehicle bodies and the causes of injury, and all findings were incorporated into the development of new models. Computer-aided simulation programmes with a three-dimensional representation of the accident sequence were used for the reconstruction. The findings the Mercedes-Benz crash researchers arrived at after their investigations were also incorporated into developing practical testing procedures and standards.

From the outset, one goal of crash testing had been to produce results that were as realistic as possible. Increasingly, therefore, the frontal collision into a rigid barrier made of old iron or concrete was replaced with an offset crash. This test, introduced in 1973, was based on the discovery that, in roughly three-quarters of all frontal collisions, the vehicles collide asymmetrically.

The 55km/h frontal crash test with 40 per cent overlap against a rigid barrier had long been one of the toughest tests for body structures, and not just for Mercedes-Benz passenger cars. Now the conditions became much more stringent: occupants were not to suffer any significant injuries after a 64km/h frontal crash test with 40 per cent overlap against the deformable barrier. From 1979, in addition to car-to-car test procedure collisions, accidents with pedestrians and cyclists/motorcyclists were also studied.

Front-end testing at the new safety centre at Sindelfingen.

Side-impact testing of a W116.

simulations of the acceleration forces that occur when a vehicle crashes. An internal company development allowed the collision- and vehicle-specific acceleration characteristics to be recreated almost exactly. However, it was just as important to know how the safety measures implemented in the vehicles performed in practice on the roads. The real-life crash events that had been recorded in detail since 1969 were therefore systematically analysed. This process brought valuable new findings for further safety developments in passenger cars. In particular, it was found that the frontal collision that was legally required as a safety test for passenger cars is actually a relatively rare occurrence. More often, collisions were asymmetric, or 'offset', with vehicles generally being hit in the corner areas. A design allowing for offset loads required additional reinforcement in the passenger cell area. These findings led to new and more realistic test-

ing methods, which were of critical importance for the development of future Mercedes-Benz vehicles.

1971–74 ESV (Experimental Safety Vehicles) programme

Experimental vehicles also played a key role in safety research. From 1971 to 1974, Mercedes-Benz took part in the international ESV (Experimental Safety Vehicles), launched in 1970 by the US Department of Transportation. As part of the programme, various automakers around the world built fifteen prototypes as test vehicles for the safe car of the future. The aim was to build cars that met the strictest requirements in terms of active and passive safety, with the goal of improving passenger cars in accordance with the safety criteria of the US National Highway Traffic Safety Administration. The specifications required a minimum risk of injury for passengers in a fron-

The ESV 05, the first publicly presented test vehicle.

tal collision at 80km/h against a rigid barrier, in a frontal collision at 120km/h with another vehicle, in a side impact with another vehicle at 50km/h, in a rear-end collision with another vehicle at 120km/h and in a rollover situation. The developments were validated in crash tests.

Mercedes-Benz presented the experimental safety vehicle ESF 05 to the public in 1971, followed in 1972 by the ESF 13. Both experimental vehicles met the ESV specifications from the US Department of Transportation and in particular the requirements for occupant protection in a frontal collision at 80km/h. (Note: ESF stands for Experimental Safety Vehicle. This is a translation of the German ESF acronym, which means Experimental-Sicherheitsfahrzeug.) The ESF 05 was one of the main attractions at the first international safety conference, hosted in 1971 by Mercedes-Benz in Sindelfingen, attended by safety engineers and researchers from all over the world.

The first ESV vehicles from Stuttgart were roughly 50 per cent heavier than the base model, the Mercedes-Benz 250 (W114 series), which drove up fuel consumption and emissions. In a bid to overcome these issues, Mercedes-Benz drew up its own specifications and focused on occupant protection at what it considered the most relevant speeds (between 50 and 80km/h), using a European-designed three-point safety belt.

The second international ESV conference was held in Sindelfingen in 1973. The ESF 22 vehicle presented in that year provided protection at 65km/h, but was still around 20 per cent heavier than the base vehicle from the Mercedes-Benz

S-Class (W116 series). Two years later, the most recent ESV from Stuttgart was the ESF 24, which was also based on the W116, but weighed only 10 per cent more than the production vehicle. Presented in June 1974, it offered the protective performance of the production vehicles, but the front section was modified to research design solutions for a frontal collision at 65km/h against a rigid barrier. A development report in 1975 stated that, in the ESF 24, Mercedes-Benz had achieved an 'optimum compromise between the original ESV requirements and our current production cars'.

Mercedes-Benz used the ESV phase to consolidate its lead in the field of passive safety. A veritable stream of Mercedes-Benz safety innovations, which were gradually brought to production standard, date from this time. Development of the airbag, which began in 1968, was stepped up during the ESV era. This was found to provide better protection for occupants than the seat belt, reducing further the risk of injury in serious frontal collisions. In this area again, Mercedes-Benz unquestionably played a pioneering role.

The principal safety features of the Mercedes-Benz ESV from that time have been integral components of series production for decades:

- Driver and passenger seats with integrated belt anchorages (in other words, the belts were fully fixed to the seat).
- Head restraints for all occupants.
- Three-point inertia-reel seat belt.

Development History of DAIMLER-BENZ Safety Vehicle

ESF 03
Presented on May 26, 1971
Specifications:
Frontal impact against fixed barrier **80 km/h**
Side impact against fixed pole 25 km/h

ESF 05
Presented on Oct. 26, 1971
Specifications:
Frontal impact against fixed barrier **80 km/h**
Frontal impact against fixed pole 80 km/h
Side impact against fixed pole 25 km/h
Side impact against fixed barrier 25 km/h
Rear-end impact 80 km/h
Drop test 0.5 m

ESF 13
Presented on May 31, 1972
Specifications:
Frontal impact against fixed barrier **80 km/h**
Frontal impact against fixed pole 80 km/h
Side impact against fixed pole 25 km/h
Side impact against fixed barrier 25 km/h
Rear-end impact 80 km/h
Drop test 0.5 m

ESF 22
Presented on March 13, 1973
Specifications:
Frontal impact against fixed barrier **65 km/h**
Frontal impact against fixed pole 50 km/h
Side impact against fixed pole 20 km/h
Side impact against vehicle 35 km/h
Rear-end impact 50 km/h
Oblique impact with moving barrier 65 km/h
Drop test 0.5 m

ESF 24
Presented on June 3, 1974
Specifications:
Frontal impact against fixed barrier **65 km/h**
All other impact modes
Correspond to Mercedes-Benz
S-Class safety level

The ESF development programme.

- Belt tensioners.
- Belt force limiters.
- Airbags.
- An especially rigid passenger cell with optimized front-end, rear and side structures.
- Safety steering wheel.
- Improvements to the vehicle to protect pedestrians and cyclists/motorcyclists.

Until the introduction of the standard three-point inertia reel seat belt, in 1973, the item remained an optional extra. When it began installing seat belts as standard equipment, Mercedes-Benz was well in advance of its legal obligations. Car manufacturers were required by law to install seat belts as standard on front seats from 1 January 1974, and the compulsory wearing of seat belts for drivers was introduced two years later, on 1 January 1976.

THE 1980S

A 1997 Mercedes-Benz brochure (60 Years of Crash Testing: On a Collision Course on Behalf of Safety) described the decade in these terms:

> All the findings arrived at up until then were now incorporated in a set of Mercedes-Benz internal safety specifications that went far beyond the legal requirements for passenger cars. Many of these safety developments that began in the ESV (Experimental Safety Vehicle) era, such as belt tensioners and airbag, have now entered series production.

The S-Class of the time (W 126) was the first series in the world that incorporated many of these innovations and before any other automobile in the world it was designed to meet the strict requirements of an asymmetric frontal collision.

Following the 126 S-Class, Mercedes-Benz also designed the compact class (201 series, the Mercedes 190, also known as the 'Baby Benz'. It was launched in December of 1982, until from 1993 when it was marketed as the C-Class), the mid-range class (124 series – built from 1985–1996) and the SL Roadster (129 series, built from 1989–2001) were all built to withstand a frontal offset collision. The superiority of this design was confirmed not only by actual crash events, but also in comparisons with competitor vehicles. A major test series, in which different competitor makes were tested in a realistic 40 per cent offset crash under exactly identical conditions (collision speed, vehicle mass, overlap) to the Mercedes-Benz passenger cars, clearly demonstrated that compliance with legal regulations offers no guarantee that all cars are equally safe.

Mercedes-Benz therefore continued consistently with the policy it had adopted with the offset barrier test, whereby all of their vehicles were primarily designed to meet on-road requirements rather than simply to comply with legal regulations. This insight also led to corresponding procedures for internal testing being drawn up, in the form of safety specifications for the rear, side and roof structures. Close collaboration was needed between test engineers and their colleagues in accident analysis in order to achieve realistic testing procedures and sensible improvements in the field of accident research. Having an exact reconstruction was extremely important for the interpretation of real-life crashes, so that many styles of accident had to be reproduced to validate the corresponding calculation methods used.

Since 1980, accident research also included accidents involving pedestrians and cyclists/motorcyclists in its analyses, and experts were employed in 'crash simulation calculation departments' to assist with these many varied accident tests; this allowed many variant solutions under consideration to be tested in advance, so that only those which are most promising need to be improved further in experiments. In the first occupant simulations, dummies were replaced by computer multi-body systems, and were then followed by

The 126 S-Class was the first car to meet the strict requirements for off-set collisions.

Even rollover crash tests were carried out in the new Sindelfingen safety centre.

BELOW: **Mercedes conducted 'real-life' accident analysis over many years.**

the first crash calculations using complete vehicle models from the E-Class at that time (124 series).

In 1987, Mercedes-Benz introduced a new type of test, representing real-life accidents on the road. The vehicle-to-vehicle check allowed for extensive testing that involved variable differences in vehicle speeds of up to 90km/h. Vehicle-to-vehicle tests allow conclusions to be drawn regarding activation compatibility, meaning that when transferred to the real-life accident event, for example, two vehicles colliding with one another can each activate the protection devices provided in the event of an accident (for example crumple zone, airbags etc).

From the mid-1980s, all Mercedes-Benz passenger cars were thoroughly refined and tested in terms of rollover safety, too, until such times as they not only met but surpassed the strict requirements set out in the safety specifications. In the case of closed vehicles, this was generally achieved by having a high-strength roof structures, as well as a roof frame, all of which were designed to absorb the load paths experienced in the event of the vehicle rolling over and maintain the integrity of the survival space. This design was, of course, more difficult to implement in open vehicles, since much of the roof structure is missing. Maintenance of the survival space was therefore ensured by development of extremely stiff front firewall and screen frame pillars, and the first ever automatically deployed roll bar systems. The R129 SL Roadster of 1989 was the first such vehicle to employ this life-saving addition.

THE 1990S

Refining the Test Methods

As a further development of the offset barrier test, studies were carried out on collisions with double offset barriers, each with a different geometry. A different approach offered a closer approximation to the damage pattern in real-life crashes: the first offset frontal collision test against a deformable barrier was conducted in 1992. An aluminium barrier with a honeycomb structure was used as the deformation element, corresponding to the average front-end rigidity in US vehicle segments up to the minivan. This was the start of another important development phase.

In 1993, this type of test – with 50 per cent overlap and at a speed of 60km/h – became the new Daimler-Benz standard. The E-Class, launched in 1995 (210 series saloon, built from 1995 to 2002, estate from 1996 to 2003), was the first Mercedes-Benz passenger car designed to meet the requirements of this kind of test.

For European car tests, the structure of the deformable barrier was significantly improved by incorporating test results from the Sindelfingen safety centre. This meant the offset test method could then be refined still further. After 1995, all Mercedes-Benz passenger cars were developed using the legally required testing method, which became compulsory only after October 1998.

The yardstick for Mercedes-Benz was always the consistent application of its own safety philosophy, in other words to make test procedures correspond exactly to actual crash events. The offset test as a new European test procedure was a crucial step towards realistic accident testing.

Side-impact testing with a deformable barrier became a standard design criterion when the C-Class was developed

When not in use, the safety bar – a U-shaped high-strength foam-padded steel tube – was deposited in front of the soft-top compartment, closing off the rear compartment towards the back. In case of an imminent rollover, the sensor-controlled bar would be electromagnetically triggered, raised into position by the force of pre-compressed springs within 0.3 seconds, and secured by pawls.

THE 1991 S-CLASS: NEW SAFETY STANDARDS

When the S-Class (140 series) premiered in March 1991 at the Geneva Motor Show, Mercedes-Benz demonstrated that, once again, it was setting new standards with its innovations for passive safety.

Crumple zone
- A massive front axle carrier provided additional protection for the footwell, even in frontal collisions with a small overlap.
- Additional support for the tried-and-tested forked longitudinal member in the form of a front cross-member.

Passenger cell
- Higher level of protection in frontal and side-on collisions, thanks to reinforced pillars and floor assembly.
- Improved safety steering column with even less backward movement in the event of a frontal collision.

Restraint systems
- Automatic belt-height adjustment, connected to the longitudinal adjustment for the seat.
- Seat-belt buckle and belt-end fitting secured to the seat.
- Increased acceptance of the seat belt, thanks to enhanced comfort in wear: the seat-belt strap is almost unnoticeable, thanks to the inertia reel system.
- Standard driver airbag, and at a later stage also a standard front-seat passenger airbag, plus belt tensioners on the front seats.

W140 had an extremely high degree of extra strengthening in all impact-vulnerable areas.

Impact-vulnerable areas were compound connected to enable transference of impact energy.

(202 series, launched in June 1993 as the successor to the popular 190 series). Standardized certification tests were carried out in accordance with North American regulations and with European designs. However, requirements in the internal specifications still needed to be met.

Public awareness of the importance of accident safety began to grow at this time. Car magazines and insurance companies in Germany and abroad drew up their own test standards for comparison testing, to enable them to assess the accident safety of vehicles and inform consumers about the results. A new law was passed in the USA dealing with side-impact protection, while draft legislation was prepared in Europe.

The measures implemented to increase passive safety greatly reduced the risk of injury. However, an analysis of actual crash events comparing the E-Class (123 series, built from 1975 to 1985) with subsequent models, did show that the reduction in thoracic injuries was smaller than that recorded for other types of injury. As a result, the safety strategy drawn up in 1991 introduced a new area of focus: its specific aim was to reduce the risk of chest injury to a minimum, by improving restraint systems and the body. One of the improvements included the concept of the belt force limiter being brought to production standard.

Developing the Facilities

In 1995, the foundation stone was laid for the Mercedes-Benz Technology Centre (MTC), which opened in 1998.

At the same time, the crash-testing facilities at Sindelfingen also underwent modernization. The acceleration track was extended to 95 metres, which meant that all crash-test variants would now be possible in the hall. This was particularly important for offset crashes, which occurred more frequently in real life than vehicle frontal collisions. Now, however, even frontal collisions between two vehicles could be carried out indoors, since the linear motor had been replaced by a cable winch system.

During the rebuilding work, the extension to the test facility was also given a roof, allowing tests with both passenger cars and commercial vehicles to take place whatever the weather.

High-speed film cameras were no longer used to record the tests; instead, the process was now recorded using video technology. The very high frequency of the image series remained unchanged, so that the crash tests could be analysed in detail in extreme slow motion.

Mid- to Late 1990s

The 1994 safety strategy included a modification to the call for a minimum deformation length for the vehicle front. A new concept of 'compatibility' linked the required deformation length to the weight and length of the vehicle. This made allowance for the fact that protection needed to be ensured, not only for the occupants of the Mercedes-Benz

New body designs for enhanced side and rear crash protection.

Enhance belt-tensioning systems and side-impact curtaining.

Computerized analysis for corkscrew rollover and roof strength.

vehicle, but also for those in the other vehicle in a frontal collision. This characteristic was tested in the vehicle/vehicle crash test.

New body designs were implemented, such as the ellipsoid bulkhead and the upper impact level as under-run protection. A design that offered protection against side and rear-end collisions was made binding for any new series. Enhanced belt tensioners, belt force limiters, side airbags and integral child safety seats supplemented the extensive range of restraint systems. Today, as a result of the expansion to the test programme and the wide range of models and variants, over 500 crash tests are conducted each year, as well as a variety of parts tests at the Sindelfingen safety centre.

In 1994, trial-and-error testing of offset rear-end collisions against a deformable barrier was performed for the first time. The load exerted on the rear-end structure was much more realistic than it had been with a rigid mobile barrier. Following these first forays, this type of test was adopted as a design criterion when developing new models. The aim was to achieve a homogeneous stiffness distribution across the entire rear area, to facilitate a favourable distribution of forces in the event of an asymmetric collision.

Similarly, the test methods used for vehicle rollover were adjusted according to the specific requirements. If necessary, for example, the corkscrew rollover test could be performed in addition to the side rollover. In this situation, the vehicle was subjected to greater translational force in addition to the rotational force exerted. The aim was to obtain parameters for the design of the roll-bar sensors, in addition to information about the structural behaviour.

By 1997, the 28th anniversary of accident research at the company, around 3,000 accidents had been investigated. All the information was stored in a database, allowing it to be evaluated according to certain criteria. One typical evaluation that s carried out by safety researchers seeks to represent the injury severity. This is classified on the MAIS scale (Maximal Abbreviated Injury Scale), which identifies the severity (from 1 = slight injury to 6 = fatal injury) according to the threat to life. With the help of such representations, safety measures that have been implemented in vehicles over the years can be evaluated in terms of their efficacy. The results show an impressive reduction in very serious and fatal injuries to drivers in high-speed frontal collisions.

CHAPTER THREE

THE PROTAGONISTS

HERMANN AHRENS

Born on 14 March 1904 in Uslar, Hermann Ahrens was to become one of the outstanding vehicle designers of his era. The basis for this ability was provided by an extremely solid technical education: Following an apprenticeship as a fitter, Ahrens trained as an engineering draughtsman, studied mechanical and electrical engineering in the 1920s in Bingen and Varel, and graduated with distinction.

After roles at the D-Werke in Berlin-Spandau and the Horch factory in Zwickau, Ahrens joined Daimler-Benz AG on 12 September 1932, where he took charge of the special vehicle production unit at the Sindelfingen plant. He had come to the attention of the Sindelfingen plant manager, Dr Wilhelm Haspel, over the course of the various popular Concours d'Élégance that took place around that time. The mighty Ahrens-designed Horch cars had won prizes for their appearance in Nice, Wiesbaden and Baden-Baden.

During his time in the special vehicle production unit, Ahrens himself designed or oversaw the design of the body shells for such outstanding models as the 380 (W22), 500K (W29), 540K (W29 and W24), the Grand Mercedes (W07 and W150), G4 (W31), 600 (W148 and W157) and the off-road sports models 170 (W15), 200 (W21), 170VS (W136), 230 (W143 and W153).

Hermann Ahrens was appointed head of the newly created special vehicle production unit at Sindelfingen in 1932. His key area of responsibility was the bodywork design of Mercedes-Benz's luxury-class models.

Ahrens in the special vehicle production unit (around 1939).

After the war and until his retirement in the late 1970s, Ahrens headed up the team developing bus and commercial vehicle bodies, while also dedicating himself to the design of the exclusive Mercedes-Benz 300 and 300 S passenger car models.

One vehicle was seldom the same as the next, particularly when it came to the exclusive models in the special class. Even if they sometimes looked the same, or very similar, from the outside, the interior details differed significantly, as each car was appointed to the individual specification of its purchaser. Among them were a few vehicle bodies which, to look at, did not have what had by then become the expected appearance of a Mercedes-Benz luxury car.

Hermann Ahrens worked not only on passenger cars, but also on commercial vehicles. In the early 1940s he designed a bus, which, with its flowing lines and angled radiator, differed significantly in shape from the convention at the time. The Second World War prevented the building of this 4.5-tonne vehicle, but a slightly modified version of it did come on to the market in 1949. From 1943 onwards, Ahrens, as head of the special commission on vehicle bodies, had also become the father of angular truck cabs built out of wooden planks. Known as 'standardized army cabs', these were built without using any steel.

Like many engineers of the time, Ahrens' departure from Daimler-Benz AG in 1945 was dictated by legislation imposed by the Allied Control Council. He worked initially in the field of interior architecture before being taken on again on 1 April 1949, at Haspel's urging, as head of development for bus and commercial vehicle bodies and for special assignments. Among these were the larger passenger car models 300 (W186, later W189) and 300 S (W188).

Ahrens' period of responsibility as far as buses were concerned covered the transition to self-supporting vehicles with flush-mounted and rear-mounted engines and, in terms of trucks, the design of the short-nosed and cab-over-engine models through to the concept for the COE generation of trucks that was built from 1973 until 1996. It was Ahrens who introduced a second 'Mercedes face' to the commercial vehicle range, one with more pronounced horizontal styling elements as first seen on the successful O 321 H model, to add to the familiar front end with the classic Mercedes radiator - so contributing to the widespread familiarity of this new characteristic feature of Mercedes-Benz vehicles.

Hermann Ahrens died on 9 November 1995 in Stuttgart.

WALTER HACKER

Born on 16 July 1905 in Patschkau (Upper Silesia), Walter Hacker's career was shaped by engineering and design work. After attending upper intermediate school in Göppingen and Ulm, he completed practical training in the fields of general mechanical engineering and metallurgy at Rheinische Metallwerke (Rheinmetall) in Düsseldorf and at Deutsche Werke (D-Werke) in Berlin-Spandau, where he got his first taste of the engineering profession. He then trained as a skilled craftsman, initially working as a machine fitter – a job that helped him appreciate the immediate connection between the use of materials and the challenges of practical work. This experience had such a formative influence that Hacker later often gave preference to prospective job applicants with a strong practical bent.

Furthering his professional training, Hacker attended the State Mechanical Engineering School in Cologne from 1924 to 1926. After graduating, he found a position at the coachwork factory of Deutsche Werke in Berlin-Spandau, where he met Hermann Ahrens, one year his senior. It was a meeting that would acquire considerable importance for his further career as a coachwork engineer and designer. When Deutsche Werke sold its coachwork unit to the American bodybuilders Ambi Budd, which also had a factory in Berlin, Hacker first went to the acquiring company. Ambi Budd was well versed in the production of all-steel bodies based on patents of its own, but, at a time when it was still common practice to build vehicles from a chassis with an auxiliary wooden frame and minimal steel work, it also stood him in good stead when he was eventually asked to join Daimler.

Hermann Ahrens had taken over as head of 'special coachbuilding' at Daimler-Benz AG in Sindelfingen in September 1932, under Wilhelm Haspel as manager of the plant. The special coachbuilding department generally still designed and produced one-off bodies built to customer specification, but both Ahrens and Haspel knew that tastes were changing. If they were to succeed and prosper, it would be necessary for them to offer bespoke design in production form.

Haspel asked Ahrens to recommend a capable design engineer for production car manufacture. Ahrens immediately recommended Walter Hacker, who began work as a body constructor at Sindelfingen on 1 October 1933. This job involved not only body styling, but also its constructional realization. Styling and design engineering were not separate disciplines in those days.

Hacker's most important pre-war designs are little known today, but they included the Mercedes-Benz models 170V (W136 series), 170H (W28), 230 (W143 and W153), 290 (W18) and 320 (W142). Hacker was esteemed for his calm and level-headed manner, both among employees and in his

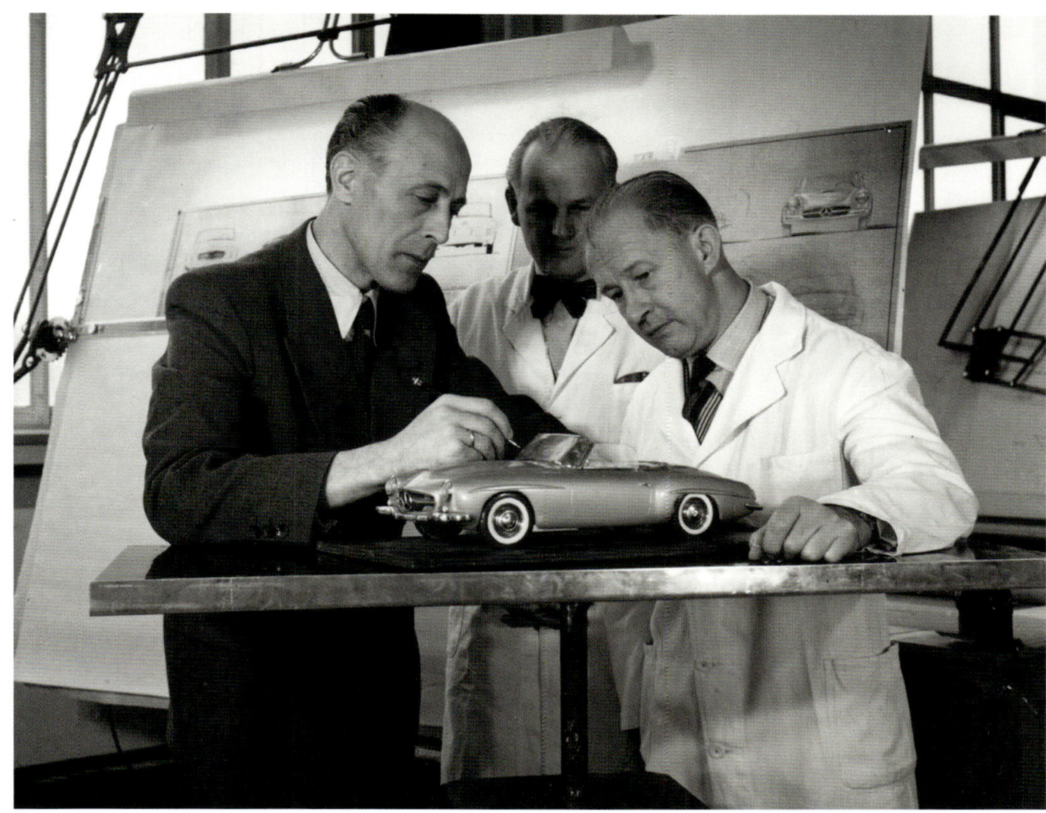

(Left to right): chief body designer Walter Häcker and design engineers Günther and Ebnet beside a 1:10 scale model of the Mercedes-Benz 190 SL (W121) in March 1955.

family, and was modest and retiring in the way he presented himself to the outside world.

Having been employed to make bodies for military vehicles during the Second World War, in 1950 Haspel appointed Hacker chief engineer for passenger car bodies. In this work he was responsible also for the production body of the Mercedes-Benz 190 SL (W121 I), again a little known fact. The vehicle was presented in 1954 and went on sale a year later with marked changes in design compared with the original version. Hacker's design was a fundamental part of the great success enjoyed subsequently by the SL model series. In particular, the 190 SL, as the first 'volume-built' SL, owes much of its huge success to the winning proportions of its body.

Hacker was appointed department head for passenger car body design and was given the title of departmental director in 1937. He went on to be manager for the Sindelfingen plant in 1950 and then in 1955, he was appointed department director for the entire passenger car body design department. During the course of his work, 120 patents in the field of body design were registered in his name.

Hacker retired after thirty-seven years of service with Daimler-Benz on 30 September 1970. He died on 24 December 1989 at his home in Aidlingen.

FREIDRICH GEIGER

Born at Süssen on the edge of the Swabian Alb on 24 November 1907, Friedrich Geiger first trained as a cartwright before studying coach design. Given that most bodies at the time consisted of a wooden auxiliary frame planked with sheet metal, this was a logical and consistent career path. On 10 April 1933, Geiger joined the special coachbuilding department at the Sindelfingen factory, where the bodybuilding approach was practised for all vehicles, including the individual creations that customers had mounted on a chassis. All-steel bodies were not introduced by Daimler-Benz until 1938 in the Mercedes-Benz 230 (W153 series).

At the Sindelfingen coachbuilding department, Geiger was able to demonstrate his double talents, both as engineer and as a person with a sense of aesthetics and proportion. Among

Freidrich Geiger at the age of 25.

the designs that originated on his drawing board were the body of the Special Roadster version of the famous 500K/540K models (W29) and the specially armoured saloons for the Grand Mercedes (W07 and W150) and the 540K. He also gained a reputation as a man of iron discipline and rigour, with a routine that began with an early-morning one-hour swim at the mineral spa in Bad Cannstatt before starting work at Sindelfingen at 7am. It is fair to say that his colleagues viewed this extreme self-discipline in different ways.

Geiger really came into his own after the Second World War, in the 1950s, when he built up and managed what became the styling department of body testing unit in Sindelfingen. There, he was working alongside Karl Wilfert, the artist, visionary engineer and driving force for passive safety.

One major, if not his most important, achievement was the Mercedes-Benz 300 SL (W198), the famed Gullwing, presented in New York in 1954. Only a year later, Geiger was designing the first bodies for the future 300 SL Roadster, introduced at the Geneva Motor Show in 1957. His design for the luxury car of the W111 series beat studies submitted by colleagues Hermann Ahrens and Walter Hacker. He succeeded in producing a design of timeless elegance in

Geiger started designing the W198 roadster even before the release of the W198 'Gullwing'.

Geiger's concave design carried on to the R107, but it was not easy to mould the concave boot lids.

the coupé variant of the 220 SE and 300 SE models (W111/W112), which was initially presented in 1961 as the 220 SE. In its formal finality, this coupé attained a great significance in Geiger's creative work. The Mercedes-Benz 600 (W100) with its angular, restrained design idiom was also his work. The heavy use of chrome was more to the taste of the board of management members responsible for development (Fritz Nallinger and, later, Hans Scherenberg), but the composed and clear lines of the luxury vehicles of the W108/109 series and the upper-intermediate range W114/115 series also revealed Geiger's own determining influence. Geiger was especially proud of the coupé of the W114 series, a car he himself drove for many years.

The body of the Mercedes-Benz 230 SL (W113), the successor to the 190 SL (W121 I), also took shape under Geiger's direction, while the Pagoda roof was championed by the engineering duo of Béla Barényi and Karl Wilfert and its design realized by Paul Bracq. Other Geiger creations that are considered classics today include both the SL and SLC models of the R/C107 series and the W116-series S-Class, along with the E-Class predecessor W123. One characteristic feature of the SL of the R107 series is the logical mirroring of the concave roof shape in the rear boot lid. This was also

Freidrich Geiger retired on 31 December 1973.

a Geiger creation, which, as future chief engineer Werner Breitschwerdt recalled, resulted in a few problems at the time. The body manufacturing process did not make it easy to mould concave boot lids.

When Friedrich Geiger retired on 31 December 1973, he could claim to have decisively shaped and influenced the formal vocabulary of Mercedes-Benz passenger cars over four decades – and in particular the design idiom of the SL models built up to that time. Werner Breitschwerdt was one future chairman of the board who thought very highly of Geiger in retrospect. He would look back on Geiger's career, and acknowledge his creativity, inspirational power and ability to take a broader view.

Friedrich Geiger died at Bad Überkingen on 13 June 1996.

KARL WILFERT

Not fashion, but the best function should prevail. For in the end what is technically suitable is always beautiful.

(Karl Wilfert)

Karl Wilfert was born in Vienna on 1 July 1907, the son of an architect, and one of a creative generation of Austrian

Karl Wilfert.

Béla Barényi (right) and Karl Wilfert (left) at the IAA in 1963.

engineers to whom the early development of the European auto industry was to become much indebted.

Having passed his state examination after four years of study at the higher mechanical engineering school in Vienna, Wilfert found employment with the Steyr automobile factory AG, where he also got to know a certain Béla Barényi. His next move was to become head of the body repair department of the Viennese Mercedes-Benz GmbH in 1929, and then, in the autumn of the same year, he joined the experimental department of the Daimler-Benz plant in Sindelfingen as assistant to chief designer Hans Nibel. In February 1933, he was promoted to head of the experimental department, the single vehicle body department, the assembly department of large production cars and the body and repair department.

Appointed chief engineer in 1940, Karl Wilfert was also temporarily employed in engine construction for aircraft engines and as head of the Schwäbisch-Gmünd repair shop.

After the war, he headed the experimental department of the Sindelfingen plant, which was extended in 1955 by a stylist department. As the head of development bodies and, later, director of all body development departments in Sindelfingen, Karl Wilfert belonged to the genius group of Fritz Nallinger and Hans Scherenberg of the engineering group and Friedrich Geiger and Béla Barényi. Together, these men shaped the constructive profile that would be associated with Mercedes-Benz vehicles for ever.

Dr Wilfert retired at the end of 1973 and died just three years later, in 1976.

BÉLA BARÉNYI

Time and again in the history of a company, the journey into the world of tomorrow is characterized by people who are among the most brilliant heads of their time. Béla Barényi was one such person.

Born on 1 March 1907 in the Austrian Hirtenberg, he achieved an excellent degree in technical engineering in Vienna, then worked for several companies as a designer and inventor in Austria, Germany and France. However, twice in his early life, the analytic thinker was a member of the growing army of the unemployed. In 1938 and for the second time, Barényi sent an application to the chief designer of Daimler-Benz, Max Wagner. Again, he received a 'No positions available' letter. After almost another year

Béla Barényi at 25 years old.

of job searching, he contacted his former colleague Karl Wilfert, with whom he had worked at Steyr in Austria. In late 1938, Wilfert, director of development for car bodies and later director of passenger car development managed to get Barényi an interview with Wilhelm Haspel. He warned him not to talk for more than two minutes: 'Important people do not have unlimited time, some are also hard to listen to and Dr Haspel is well known for not suffering fools who speak incessantly.'

The interview started well, with Barényi declining the seat that was offered, then Dr Haspel asked the young engineer about the future of the automobile. At this point, Barényi forgot Wilfert's advice and allowed his passion to take over. For twenty minutes, he hardly drew breath, telling Dr Haspel exactly what was wrong with the cars of the time as well as pointing out the shortcomings of the Daimler-Benz styling department.

Fortunately, Haspel was convinced. He immediately introduced the unemployed visionary to the design team, explain-

Béla Barényi in at the deep end in 1939.

Béla Barényi was admitted to the Automotive Hall of Fame in September 1994 in Detroit, Michigan.

ing his decision with the legendary words: 'A house like Daimler-Benz cannot live from hand to mouth. Mr Barényi, you think fifteen to twenty years ahead. You will be put under a "bell jar". From this moment forward everything you invent comes directly into the patent department.' He was given free rein for his creative thinking, and was allowed to develop his ideas, independent of the constraints of serial development.

One thing that Mercedes-Benz and Béla Barényi had in common was a passion for safety. These were the days when car manufacturers carefully avoided using the term; particularly in the post-war period, nobody wanted to be reminded about the dangers of driving. The topic was viewed as a sales killer, even as late as the 1970s, but Béla Barényi was not deterred by this.

Barényi was one of the most exceptional inventors of the twentieth century, and a pioneer of passive safety. More than 2,500 patents originated from him, some of which have saved thousands of lives and still set the automotive standard today. After his retirement in 1972, and particularly after the death of his wife in 1980, Barényi devoted himself to building up his personal archives. He had already received the Rudolf Diesel medal from the German Inventors' Association in 1967, and even after his retirement he received numerous awards and honours in recognition of his life's work. In 1981 he was awarded the Aachen and Munich Prize for technology and the applied sciences, and in 1986 the Deutsche Museum in Munich honoured him with a special exhibition entitled 'Barényi and his design concept of 1925 for the people's car [*Volkswagen*] of the future'. This was followed by another Deutsche Museum exhibition the following year, on the occasion of his 80th birthday, entitled 'Béla Barényi, Automotive Pioneer'. In 1987 he received the Badge of Honour of the city of Sindelfingen and the freedom of the town of Terracina. His portrait was placed in the Inventors' Gallery at the German Patent Office in Munich, and the Museum of Technology in Vienna devoted several display cases to his achievements. It was a fitting gesture of recognition from the country of his birth. He was also appointed as an emeritus professor in Austria in 1989, and received the city of Baden's Culture Prize for outstanding scientific achievements. In 1991 he even became the main character in a Mercedes-Benz publicity film on automotive safety.

The father of passive safety, who chattered charmingly and with impressive energy for his convictions, died on 30 May 1997 at the age of 90.

FRITZ NALLINGER

Fritz Nallinger was born in Esslingenon on 6 June 1898, the fourth child of Daimler-Motoren-Gesellschaft board member Friedrich Nallinger. As a young student, he spent time working at Benz & Cie on aircraft engines, and he later gained experience as a pilot when serving in the First World War. At the end of the war he moved directly into mechanical engineering at the Karlsruhe University.

Nallinger's professional career began in 1922, when he joined Benz & Cie officially, in the design office. Carl Benz was still focusing on racing and sports driving and Nallinger took part in many reliability tests with remarkable success. His work in motor racing taught him much about safe and reliable construction techniques and furthered his experience with swing-axle suspension and diesel engineering. In 1924 he moved to Untertürkheim as an experienced engineer and continued his work with diesel engines, mainly in the truck department. Working closely with W. Lippart of Bosch, they advanced the technology of pumps and injectors and introduced the first 'glow-plug' technology.

After the merger between Benz and Daimler in 1924, Nallinger took over the management of the entire experimental facility, overseeing marine, rail, aircraft and heavy vehicle engine development. When Ferdinand Porsche vacated his chair in 1928, due to disagreements with the board, Hans Nibel took over the position of chief designer. As his closest associate, Nallinger had the opportunity to put forward his own ideas on future vehicle and engine concepts, in particular on development work and test operation. This led to the first experiments with the Vollschwingachsen chassis, which

came to be used in 1931 for the first time in the 'small Mercedes' type 170. Later, his experimental work with Arthur Berger and Albert Friedrich produced the first-ever direct injection gasoline aircraft engine which produced 1000 bhp.

In 1935, Nallinger was appointed chief technical officer for large engine construction, just as demand was growing for bigger and more efficient engines leading up to the Second World War. In 1940 he became a full member of the executive board, responsible for the entire Daimler-Benz programme. He proved versatile and highly competent in this position.

Nallinger's first public success came in 1937, when he achieved several world records for his aircraft engines. In 1939 he achieved a number of airspeed records with Heinkel and Messerschmitt aircraft. In 1936 his fuel-efficient, high-speed diesel engines had been used for the first time in a saloon car in the type 260 D, and the LZ 129 'Hindenburg'

Fritz Nallinger at the age of 24.

Front 2nd on left Rudolf Uhlenhaut, Hans Scherenberg and Dr Fritz Nallinger Italian grand Prix in Monza, 5. September 1954.

had been the first airship to be fitted with sixteen-cylinder versions of his engines. During the early war period of 1939 to 1942, he developed the DB600 series of engines, the first X-shaped inline engine with twenty-four cylinders and rotary valve control, which went on to develop close to 2500 bhp (1800Kw). During Nallinger's tenure until 1945, 100,000 aircraft engines were produced.

When the piston engine in the aircraft was to be replaced by the turbine, Nallinger created the special engines department, under the auspices of Karl Leist, to develop a two-circuit jet engine and a propeller turbine. Although it did not come to fruition during the war period, it did go on to be the foundation of today's modern twin circuit gas turbine engines

In 1940, Nallinger was appointed a director in research and development, and in 1941 he became a full member of the board.

From the end of the Second World War until the beginning of 1948, Nallinger's mandate with Daimler was suspended because of a special commission from the French government for the further development of large aircraft turbine engines at J. Szydlowski in Pau. However, by May 1948 he had resumed his duties as a board member and technical director of Daimler-Benz AG, now with overall responsibility for design, testing and development of all vehicle lines of the house.

The following years of his tenure saw many technical milestones, including self-supporting bodies, sub-frame technology, single-joint pendulum rear axle, recirculating ball steering, valve-controlled short-stroke engines, fuel injection, automatic transmission and disc brakes. Alongside these developments, a large number of new passenger car models were developed that had a significant impact on international automotive engineering.

Rudolf Uhlenhaut (left) and Prof. Dr Fritz Nallinger with the Mercedes-Benz F1 Rennwagen W196.

Fritz Nallinger and Director Karl Wilfert present the special W100 600 to Pope Paul VI in 1965.

In the 1950s, Nallinger, Hans Scherenberg and Rudolf Uhlenhaut returned the company to Grand Prix racing again and developed a new racing car, which, as a W196, became one of the most successful of the post-war epoch. In 1963 the Type W600 was introduced; a top-of-the-range model that followed the tradition of the 'big Mercedes' of the pre-war period. Most of the technical innovation had been developed by Nallinger and his team.

Fritz Nallinger frequently sent his brightest engineers to work with universities on the continuous improvement of production technology and advancements in design and construction. The aim was to achieve, through scientific and technical collaboration between scholars and engineers, what became known in the mid-1930s as *Kaizen* or 'betterment'. It had such an impact on everything that was done at Daimler-Benz that the results could still be felt many decades after Nallinger's retirement.

Fritz Nallinger retired at the end of 1965, with more than 300 patents having been made in his name. During his tenure, Daimler-Benz had developed into the world's largest manufacturer of commercial vehicles and large engines for locomotives, ships and power plants.

HANS OTTO SCHERENBERG

Professor Hans Otto Scherenberg is often described as having engineering in the blood. Born in Dresden in 1910, he grew up in Heidelberg and attended a humanistic grammar school, where he learnt the importance of self-expression through design. Fascinated by the mechanical world from a very early age, the young lad would spend much of his free time 'problem-solving' what he described as engineering issues that were not 'quite right'.

Scherenberg devoted himself to the study of mechanical engineering at the Stuttgart and Karlsruhe Colleges of Technology. As a newly graduated engineer, at the age of 25 he joined the experimental department for passenger vehicles at Daimler-Benz AG Untertürkheim, initially collaborating with Fritz Nallinger on the 260 D, the first diesel car in the world, and later on the DB600 series of aircraft engines.

For many years after this time, Scherenberg worked on questions concerning increasing power. He was engaged on the further improvement of the pre-chamber system on the diesel engine, the development and control of fuel injection in conjunction with valve-timing on aircraft engines, as well

Hans Otto Scherenberg.

as working on the development of completely new designs.

In 1942, Scherenberg was awarded a doctorate in engineering from Stuttgart University for his thesis 'Valve-timing in 4-stroke high-altitude aircraft engines'. He had achieved considerable success in obtaining higher engine power at great altitudes through the correct matching of supercharger, valve-timing and fuel injection. After the end of the war, however, on the instructions of the Allied Control Council, the work on aircraft engines had to be stopped and Scherenberg made the decision to leave Daimler-Benz AG. He worked in Dr Schnürle's engineering office where the further development of the 2-stroke engine was of prime importance. In 1946 he was collaborating with the Gutbrod-

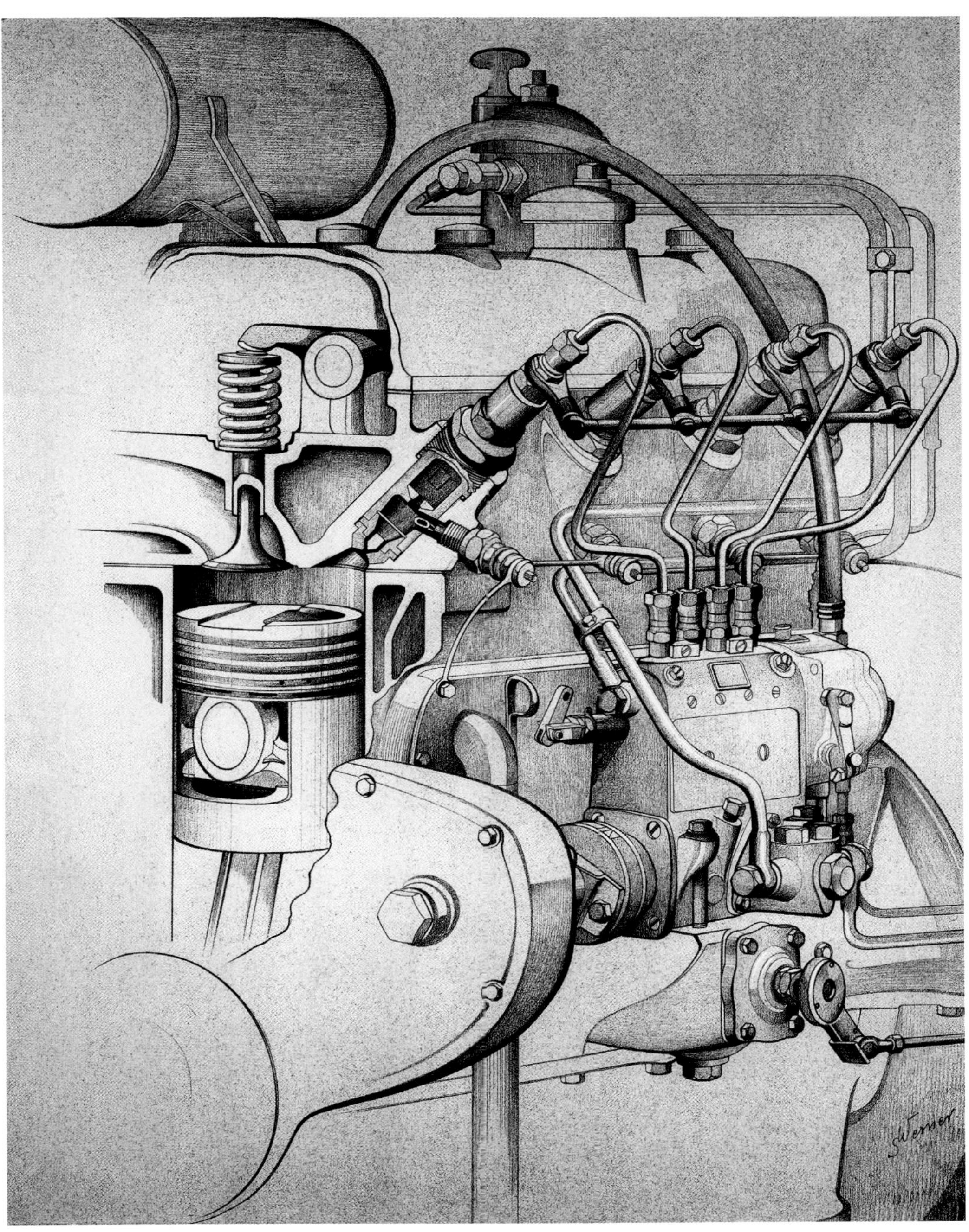

Werken in Plochingen where, two years later, he took over as head of development and manufacture. It was thanks to him and his team that the Gutbrod 'Superior' with fuel injection came on to the market. This trend-setting small vehicle was hailed by the technical world of the early 1950s for its progressive concept and design.

In 1952, Fritz Nallinger managed to entice the 41-year-old Scherenberg back to Daimler-Benz, appointing him as head of car design in Untertürkheim. It was to prove to be an extremely important period for Daimler-Benz, marked by far-reaching innovations in technology and design. As the Federal Republic began to rise from the ashes of war, and

The world's first serial-production diesel passenger car engine, the Mercedes-Benz 260 D (W138).

its economic life began to prosper once again, Daimler-Benz was able to reconfirm and emphasize its position. The models in the 180, 190 and 220a range particularly, with their self-supporting Ponton bodywork, the frame floor unit, the single joint swing axle and the sub-frame that combined the elements in the front wheel suspension, would set another trend in automobile design and have a lasting effect on the industry.

Further examples of technical progress at Daimler-Benz during this period included the racing and sports cars, with the Formula One W196, the W196S. Both had desmodromic valve control and dominated the motorsport competitions of their time. Dr Scherenberg and his team exercised great influence on these projects, particularly on the fuel-injection system fitted to the dynamic high-performance 300 SL sports car. The advantages of the system were impressively demonstrated in this vehicle, and it was subsequently fitted into the standard road model.

Appointed deputy member of the executive board in 1955, Scherenberg, was also responsible for large engine construction as well as for central development areas such as the technical data centre and the computer centre. In 1965 he succeeded Fritz Nallinger as head of all departments in the development division, and became a full member of the board of management. Difficult tasks awaited the man who was now at the head of a team comprising thousands of engineers. First, there was the completion of the 'new generation' models, which were largely the brainchild of Nallinger and were introduced in 1968. This was followed in 1972 by the launching to the public of the S-Class models, and finally by the design of the wildly successful 123 model range, which bore Scherenberg's signature, as did the SL and SLC models currently in production.

In the 1980s and 90s, the company had to determine the direction of its research, development and design. This would largely depend upon a decision as to whether development of the Wankel engine, which had started in 1960, should be continued, completed or abandoned. A decision was taken that 'safety designs' would take precedence and

this gave rise to a period of continuously increasing creativity on the part of the entire design team during the middle sixties because of more stringent official safety regulations above all, in the USA.

It must be noted that, even though Scherenberg had a great interest in vehicle safety and was instrumental in the development of the anti-lock braking system (ABS) introduced in 1970 and co-initiator of the ESV (Experimental Safety Vehicle) and the airbag, he never let go of his roots as an engine developer. He had already foreseen that mass motorization would impact the environment and intensified his work in the fields of exhaust gas purification, and alternative propulsion systems and fuels. He went on to develop the first hybrid vehicles made in 1969, the natural gas experimental bus in 1971, the 1972 electric van and the hydrogen-powered vehicles presented in 1975.

In recognition of his achievements, Scherenberg was made an honorary member of the board of the University of Karlsruhe in 1969. In 1970 he was awarded an honorary doctorate by the Technical University Berlin, and in 1973 he became honorary professor to the University of Stuttgart (in the energy technology department). On 28 October 1975, his 65th birthday, Professor Scherenberg was awarded the Grand Cross of the Order of Merit of the Federal Republic of Germany.

After thirty-five years at Daimler-Benz AG, apart from the war-related interruption, Scherenberg handed over the research and development division to his successor, chief

The frame floor unit.

Presentation of the 'New Mercedes-Benz Generation' on 9 and 10 January 1968 in Sindelfingen. Head engineer Hans Scherenberg (left) presents the new models (on the stage, from left to right) 220 D (W115), 280 S (W108) and 250 (W114).

Scherenberg presenting ESF22 at the Tokyo safety in design conference.

Werner Breitschwerdt (right) and Hans Scherenberg in 1977, on Scherenberg's retirement.

engineer Werner Breitschwerdt, who had worked in the Daimler-Benz development department for almost twenty-five years

Hans Otto Scherenberg retired on 31 December 1977 and died on 17 November 2000, just a few weeks after his 90th birthday.

WERNER BREITSCHWERDT

Werner Breitschwerdt was born on 23 September 1927 in Stuttgart. He studied electrical engineering at the Technical University of Stuttgart, passing his diplomas in 1952. After graduating, he stayed on as an assistant director of electrical systems at the university, but he was soon invited to apply to Daimler. He joined the company on 16 April 1953, to work on vehicle bodywork research at Sindelfingen.

In 1960 Breitschwerdt became head of the standard production car body design office and, in 1963, head of the car research department. On 1 May 1965 he was appointed as senior head of the department for car body research, then, on 27 July 1971, deputy director of the car division and deputy to Dr Karl Wilfert, who was head of car body development at the time. After Wilfert's retirement, Breitschwerdt took over the styling department as divisional director, on 17 December 1973, becoming department manager on 15 July 1976.

At the beginning of 1977, Breitschwerdt became a board member at Daimler-Benz and then took over the department of development and research in 1978, as successor to Hans Scherenberg.

Werner Breitschwerdt.

During Breitschwerdt's leadership, several new generations of vehicles emerged: W126, W201, R129 and W124.

Breitschwerdt made significant contributions to the commercial vehicle programme.

In appointing Werner Breitschwerdt, the supervisory board picked an engineer who not only knew his work through and through, but also had the rare ability to motivate colleagues without neglecting the human relationships that were essential to a productive creative atmosphere. Several new generations of vehicles emerged under Breitschwerdt's leadership in the development and research departments: the S-Class series W126 (1979 to 1991), the middle series W124 (1984 to 1995) and the SL series R129 (1989 to 2001). His name is also closely associated with the type 190 (W201), which came on the market in 1982. The 190s were the first models to benefit from certain new developments, such as the multi-link rear axle (*Raumlenkerachse*).

Breitschwerdt subscribed closely to the Daimler-Benz philosophy of vehicle safety and occupant protection, and was instrumental in the design and development of new assistance and safety systems in the 1970s and 1980s. The introduction of the anti-lock brake system and the airbag fell

under his remit. He also chaired the European project PRO-METHEUS (Program for European Traffic with Highest Efficiency and Unprecedented Safety), which was launched in 1986 and ran as a cooperation of several European automakers, electronics and supply companies, universities and institutes over eight years. The programme resulted in many new technologies, which were converted into concrete technical products at Mercedes-Benz, including the intelligent cruise control DISTRONIC PLUS and an automatic passenger and driver safety feature known as PRE-SAFE®.

Under his responsibility, Daimler-Benz also made further significant progress in terms of the economy and environmental friendliness of Mercedes-Benz vehicles. Breitschwerdt also made major contributions to the expansion and further development of the Mercedes-Benz commercial vehicle programme.

Breitschwerdt received a number of awards for his work, including the Grashof Commemorative Coin of the Association of German Engineers (1985); the Medal of Merit of the State of Baden-Württemberg (1991); the Order of Merit of the Land Berlin (1998); the Grand Cross of Merit of the Federal Republic of Germany (1987); the Grand Golden Badge of Honour for Meritorious Service to the Republic of Austria (1980); and the Public Service Medal of the City of Stuttgart. Finally, on 3 March 2009, Breitschwerdt was admitted to the European Automotive Hall of Fame.

PAUL BRACQ

Born in Bordeaux, Paul Bracq learnt the craft of wood sculpture at the École Boulle in Paris from 1950 to 1952. However, it was the car that really stirred the artist within, so while at the school, he also took a correspondence course with the Chambre Syndicale de la Carrosserie (the coachbuilders' guild), studying technical draughtsmanship. In 1953, he had a piece of work based on the Lancia Aurelia published in *L'Automobile* magazine. The work displayed a marked maturity, and immediately caught the eye of designer and engineer Philippe Charbonneaux, who offered him a position working on various car bodywork projects.

In October 1954, Paul Bracq was summoned to perform his three-year military service in occupied Germany. Owing to his previous work experience, he was assigned to the garage of the Air Force headquarters, where a number of beautiful German cars, including the majestic Mercedes 300 Ade-

Featured in *L'Automobile* magazine, 1953, the Lancia Aurelia model by Paul Bracq.

Philippe Charbonneaux's Salmson roadster concept by Bracq was just a little too forward-thinking and never went ahead.

The nose on the 300 models (top row) would prove remarkably prescient, finding its way on to the 2003 Mercedes-Benz SLR McLaren and its 2004 SLK sibling.

nauer, were housed. Bracq was in awe of this German vehicle manufacturer that had dragged itself up from such a low point after the war years and was now in the ascendancy, unlike its French counterparts. One day, while delivering the 300 to the maintenance department of Mercedes-Benz in Stuttgart, he took the opportunity to go to the press department on the pretext of asking for some racing posters. While there, he had a serendipitous encounter with Wilhelm von Urach, who was not only a race design engineer but also French-speaking, having spent some time working in France for Renault. Just eight days later, Bracq was invited to meet Karl Wilfert, then head of design at Mercedes.

Bracq showed Wilfert some of his studies on the Mercedes-Benz sports and racing cars. Wilfert was suitably impressed and after just a ten-minute interview he offered to hire him at the end of his militant service. Bracq was overjoyed, not only at the prospect of working for this most prestigious of brands, but also at being the first Frenchman ever to have been recruited by them.

Unfortunately, following the outbreak of the Algerian war, Bracq found himself wearing the uniform a further eighteen months. At least it gave him the time to learn German. Luckily, Karl Wilfert did not break his word and, on 1 March 1957, Bracq returned to Sindelfingen and joined the stylist unit of Mercedes as their first designer employee, on a monthly wage of 500DM.

Daimler-Benz had been relying on individuals such as Friedrich Geiger, Walter Hacker and Herman Ahrens for their recent road car designs, but this pre-war generation were now moving up the ranks. Wilfert was determined to create a styling department that could meet the rapidly evolving modern aesthetic, and Bracq was effectively its first new employee. Initially installed under Hacker, by 1959 Bracq was reporting to the quiet and considered Friedrich Geiger in the newly formed advanced styling studio. Bracq's contract also called for him to produce images for the marketing department – as well as a facility in sculpting, he was also highly skilled in the art of rendering. Geiger's team worked

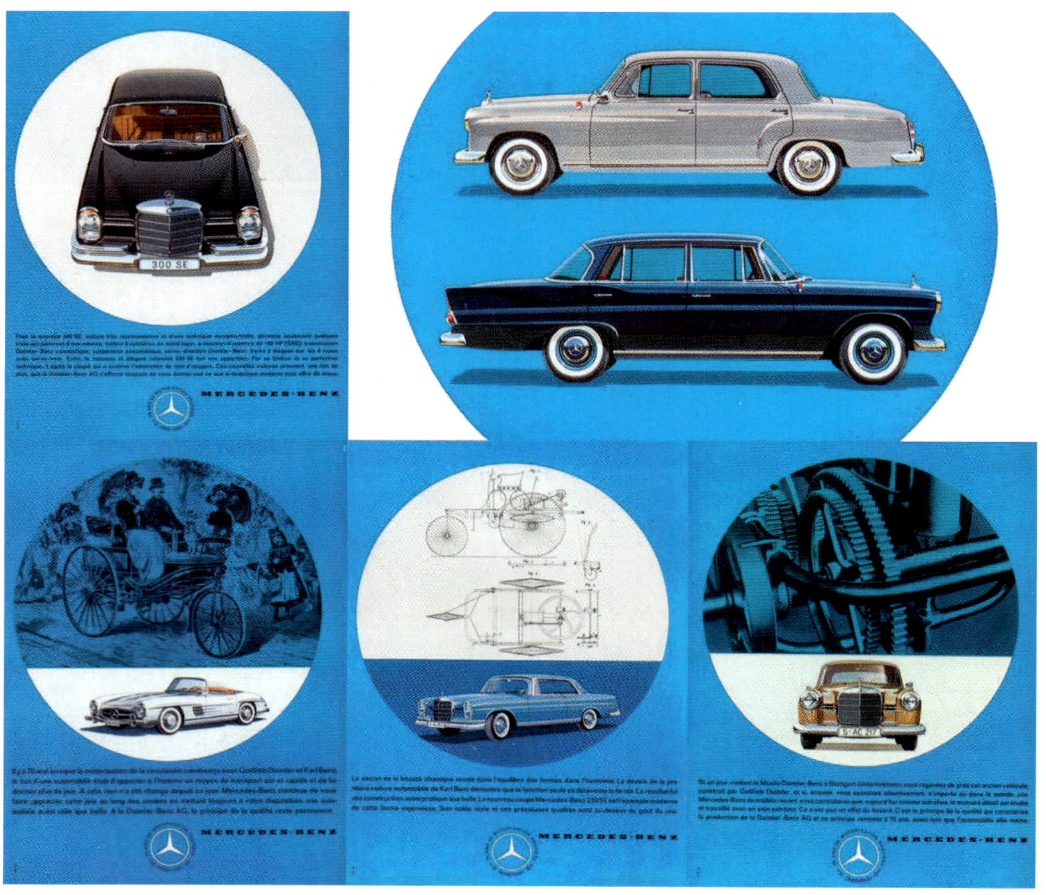

Bracq also produced artwork for the marketing department: this depicts the current range for an advertising campaign celebrating the 75th anniversary in 1961.

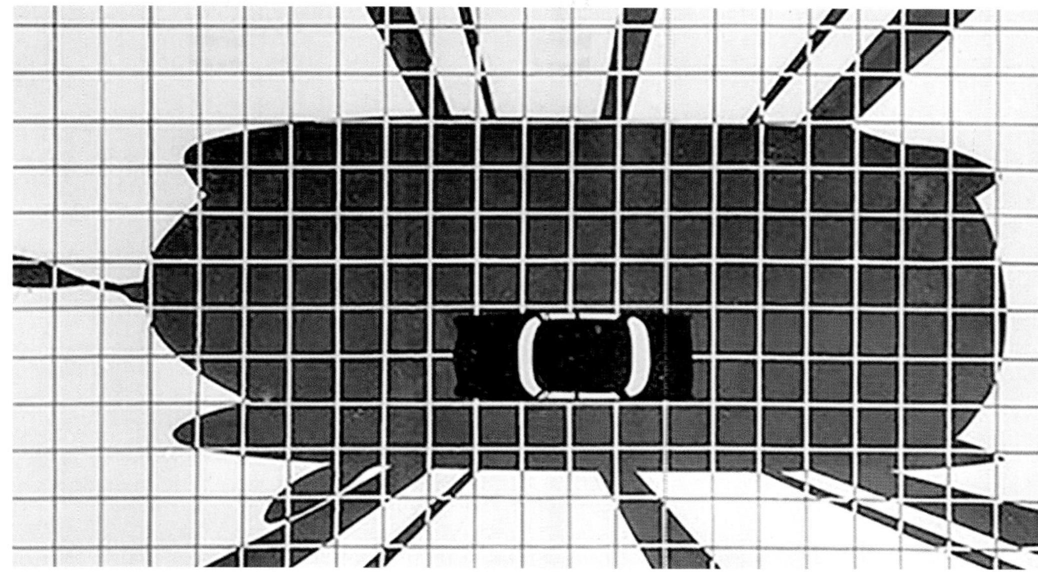

Fascinating diagram prepared by Paul Bracq, considering the sightlines of a left-hand-side driver down to the road surface.

with a remarkable sense of cohesion and efficiency. For the first time there was a palpable symbiosis between research, style and testing.

Bracq's most significant contribution to Daimler-Benz was in shaping the passenger cars of the 1960s, taking the marque's established identity and extrapolating it effortlessly into the new ranges. Each model was marked by a cleanness of line and volume, retaining the dignity of Daimler-Benz but adding perhaps a little more chic than its British rivals. In truth, all the saloons and coupés of the 1960s owed an immeasurable debt to the fintail model first seen in 1959. Shaped by Friedrich Geiger, these cars had introduced Daimler-Benz to the principles of clean, straight-through body sides and an airy, squared-off glass interior. Most distinctive was its front face: an amalgam of the upright saloon grille with the 'Lichteinheit' ovoid composite headlights from the 300 SL Roadster. Bracq would take this look and redefine Mercedes-Benz design for decades to come.

In the late 1950s, European manufacturers were looking to appeal to the demands of an ever-expanding market across the Atlantic. The use of the fintail had marked a period at Daimler-Benz when the US idiom was exerting a significant influence. With Bracq's arrival, however, it was time to stop following trends and to define the Mercedes as a Mercedes. He retained the C-pillar from the tailfin model but re-drew the trailing-edge bend at a less acute angle. More importantly, the slightly raised wing line and reverse-cant fins were gone, replaced with a gently sloping line and forward-cant

end. These shapes caused a sensation, and would define the Mercedes-Benz rear for the 1960s.

For the following W108/109 saloons, Bracq had made his mark, adhering to four self-established principles in car design: well-balanced proportions, a continuous line stem to stern along the flanks to emphasize length, wheels that fit within their well so as to appear flush with the body, and a low-set waistline with deep glazed interior above. However, his design was not just about aesthetics – Daimler-Benz was foremost a highly disciplined engineering firm. For example, safety was no longer a passing thought but had become of paramount importance.

Not long after Bracq arrived at Daimler-Benz, he found himself in discussions with Béla Barényi. For a few years, Barényi had been mulling over a concept that was forward-thinking and utterly pragmatic. In the middle of the conversation with Bracq, he grabbed a pen and scrawled a diagram of a vehicle that featured a loop bumper arrangement. At that point, it also included 'cat's ear' fins at the rear. Bracq went away and prepared some technical drawings, removing the fins but keeping the rest of concept intact.

The compact people's car did not exceed the footprint of the VW Beetle, and yet the passenger compartment could hold four in the comfort of a larger saloon. A sliding door would further limit its footprint (although this was not included on the prototype). Steering, instruments and pedals could be switched from side to side with a few hand movements. The body was built to the principles of the

While in discussion with Bracq, Béla Barényi grabbed a pen and made a first sketch of his 'pagoda' idea.

Béla Barényi's compact people's car concept.

Sketches by Bracq suggest that the compact concept was considered as a future Mercedes-Benz car.

The people's car progressed to model stage.

A drawing from June 1958 of an early **W113** design. Still in the sway of the **US** influence, it sets the proportions for the new model, albeit with over-complicated detailing.

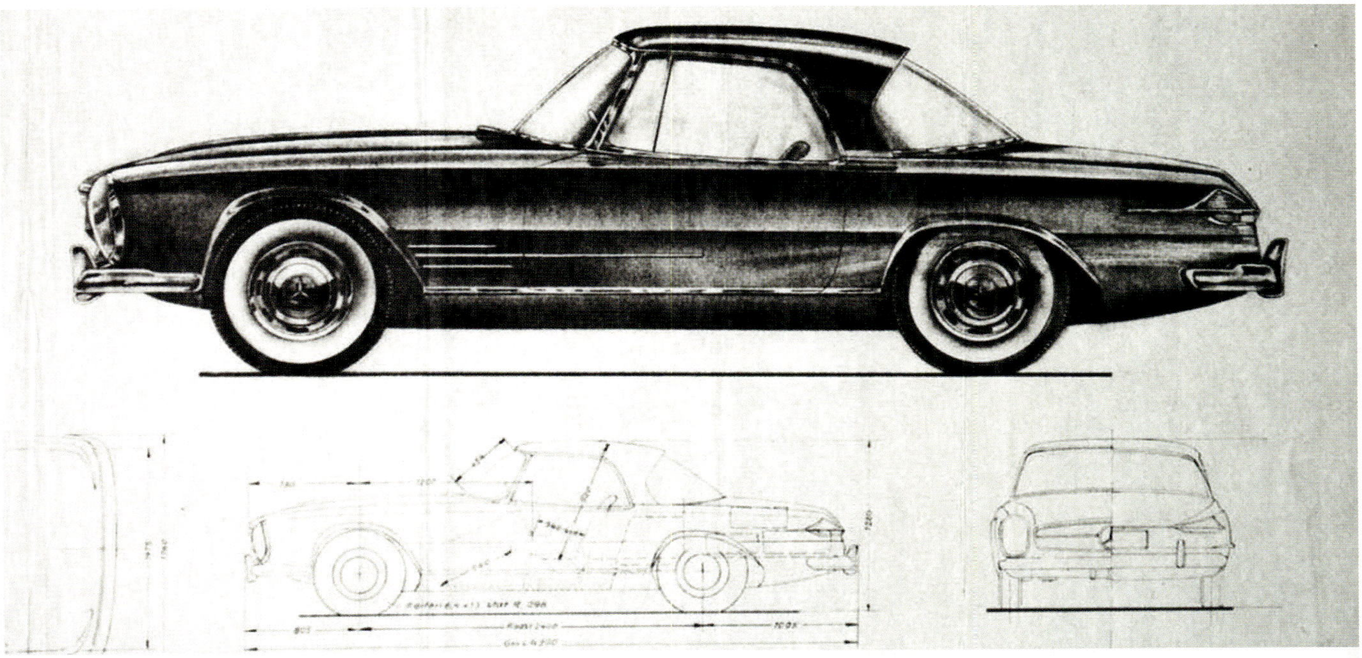

Similar-looking sketches of the **SL** replacement W113.

crumple zone and safety cell that Barényi had pioneered, and it was symmetrical front to rear, which reduced the number of parts needed for construction.

Work continued on the shape through the early 1960s and a prototype was produced. Although, ultimately, Karl Wilfert decreed that the project should be cancelled, there was one aspect that was to find its way on to other Mercedes-Benz cars. In order to maximize its space utility, Barényi had proposed a load-bearing roof for carrying luggage or perhaps even sleeping bodies. In order to strengthen this, longitudinal ridges had been applied to the roof's edges. The idea had been patented back in 1956. On the K-55, it became the first example of what quickly became known by the press as the 'Pagoda' roof.

Around the same time, Bracq had been working on a sports car – a coupé with a removable hard top – that could replace both the 300 SL and the Gullwing in one model. Even though Barényi's K-55 compact people's car had not gone into production, its curved strengthened Pagoda roof found its way on to this new car. With the 230 SL Pagoda of 1963, Bracq had created his first masterpiece – a subtle blend of classicism and avant-garde, distinguished by the finesse of its lines, and accompanied by a strong development of the large glass surface. Bright-

A similar depiction in scale-model form sitting behind Friedrich Geiger in his office. Daimler-Benz were seriously considering these shapes at this time.

Full-scale body from 1961, showing the shape close to completion. However, it is missing one small but innovative design concept from the production W113.

Paul Bracq at his drawing board.

Paul Bracq would freely sketch ideas based on other vehicles in the market.

ness, transparency and safety were among the fundamental principles of the art of Paul Bracq:

> *In a car, I always liked to see clearly to communicate better with the environment. To increase the glazed surface, I lowered the body line and the result was a safer car.*

Paul Bracq's designs began many trends in Mercedes-Benz, none more important than the assertion that beauty did not have to be sacrificed in pursuit of innovation or safety. In this respect, he was thirty years ahead of the curve; however, his extraordinary foresight would also lead to his departure from Mercedes-Benz:

> *I had a drawer full of innovative future designs all of Mercedes but Mercedes moved too slow for me. I yearned for more and my homeland was calling me.*

Bracq left Mercedes-Benz in 1967 and returned to France, where he worked on the designs for the TGV high-speed train, among other projects.

SHAPING THE BRAND THE SACCO WAY

DEVELOPMENTS IN DESIGN

From 1975 there were marked changes in the public's understanding of the car. As customers increasingly valued above all else the practical qualities of a vehicle, there was more and more interest in compact cars, hatchbacks and estates. By the mid-1980s the first people carriers were beginning to appear, offering maximum use of space and great flexibility.

In the 1970s, bright, cheerful colours such as yellow, orange, light green, light blue and red were the most popular for cars, along with beige. This was also the case for interiors. However, by the early 1980s at the latest, the bright colours had served their time. Chrome decoration was also used less frequently. Unostentatious dashboards were visible testimony to the introduction of electronics into automotive design.

The model range was expanding, but every model still had to look like a Mercedes.

At the same time, automotive manufacturers began to use new materials, presenting designers with new opportunities. It was now possible to save weight and improve aerodynamic values by producing bumpers in plastic and aluminium. As the wind tunnel played an increasingly important role – at least in Europe – the angular designs of the late 1970s and early 80s began to be replaced by slimmer, more rounded bodies with smooth surfaces and bumpers mounted closer to the body. Fusing the body and bumpers into a single entity not only created a visual impact, but also improved aerodynamics. The wedge shape was introduced at Mercedes in the S-Class from 1979 and the shape later more pronounced in the new small series, the 190, initially known familiarly as the 'Baby Benz'.

There were many more small details that pointed to a concerted effort to improve aerodynamic performance: door handles were sunk flush with the body, exterior mirrors were streamlined, gaps in bodywork were minimized and under-bodies were smoothed.

Above all, the one factor that had a decisive influence on the design of Mercedes-Benz vehicles was the decision to expand the model range – even if this was done cautiously at first. Following the 190, there was the G-model (today known as the G-Class) and, for the first time, an estate, designated the T-model. The designers were confronted with the difficult challenge of giving each model series an individual face that reflected its character and simultaneously ensured that every Mercedes was instantly recognizable as a Mercedes. In addition, every new model generation had to build a formal link with the future without neglecting its starting point. Each new Mercedes-Benz was given an unmistakable identity and revealed its good breeding at first sight. Fashionable trends were out of the question for Mercedes designers, since they lacked the ingredient that made Mercedes-Benz different: the long-term effect.

EXPANDING THE MODEL RANGE

In 1993 the challenge facing designers became even more demanding with the launch of a strategic product initiative, when Mercedes-Benz very rapidly expanded its model range and created a new brand image.

The First Estate

In 1976 Mercedes-Benz presented the successor to the Stroke Eight models and in the following year an estate (T-model) was added to the series (internal designation

The lines of the first estate car were so successful that it was comparable in terms of prestige to the saloon of the same series.

Even considering its utilitarianism, the S123 remained classily elegant.

The front was all Mercedes.

W123). This was in line with expectations of a period in which customers were increasingly demanding cars that demonstrated both practicality and flexibility. The estate received a very warm reception from the outset; it very quickly gained a reputation as the best, most robust model in the estate range. In addition, its lines were so successful that it was perceived as being comparable in terms of prestige to the saloon of the same series.

The design of the estate was closely modelled on the wedge-shaped saloon, which was longer, broader and lower than its predecessor. Even the classic Mercedes simulated radiator grille was lower so as to accommodate the wedge shape. Circular, double headlamps beneath a common glass cover flanked the radiator; the top-of-the-range models had horizontal rectangular headlamps.

Professor Dr Hans Scherenberg, at the time a member of the board of management and head of research and overall development, described the new vehicle as follows:

In the case of the new models we have attempted to create a balanced, dynamic, non-aggressive form — one that lends these vehicles a special character — by emphasizing horizontal lines both at the front and rear, suggesting a slight wedge shape from the side aspect, reducing the use of chrome trim and, in the truest sense of the term, introducing rounded lines. ...We are as unimpressed by revolutionary leaps of style as by fashionable gimmicks; stylistic continuity is a characteristic feature of the products of our company, and the lines must clearly identify kinship to the other models.

The rear showed the classic wedge-shaped stance.

Internal configuration was as important as exterior design.

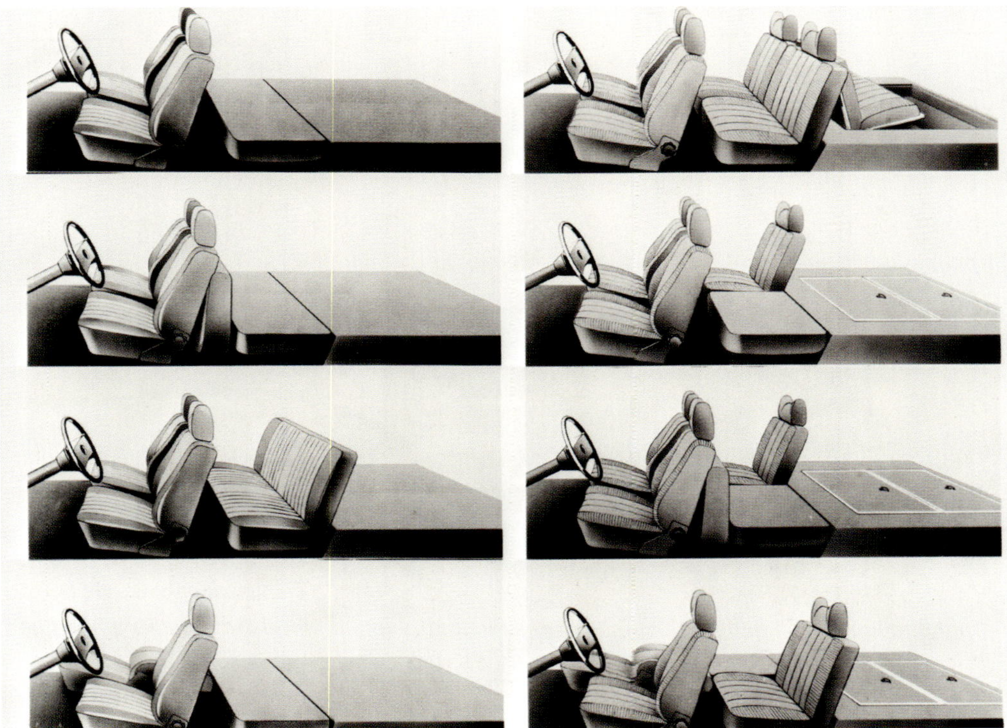

G-Class: The 4X4

Another innovation was the G-Model, which is still built today, known as the G-Class. It first appeared in 1979 and in terms of its design the Mercedes-Benz stylists had followed the requirements of an off-road vehicle. It had to afford the driver good visibility, be narrow enough for forest tracks and yet at the same time reflect a robust character. For this reason, it was decided to adopt the clear, distinctive shape that makes the Mercedes off-road vehicle so unmistakable even today. Its characteristic features included straight lines, balanced proportions of its surfaces, short overhangs and angular wings to facilitate good visibility of the road or track, and precise steering.

For the interior of the G-Class, the designers initially opted for a simple but practical and functional approach, with painted steel surfaces and minimal trim. The two-spoke steering wheel allowed the driver a clear view of the simple instrument panel with speedometer and function lights. Centrally positioned were easy-to-use push switches as well as the controls for heating and ventilation. However, right from the start of its long career, the G-Class had also been planned with some superior interior equipment, such as shaped foam elements to cover certain steel surfaces.

G-Model design.

In spite of its orientation towards the practical and the functional, the G-Class displayed a strong formal aesthetic. With its clear lines and harmonious forms, it was clear at first sight that this car would rise above fashion and resolutely go its own way – as indeed it has done now for nearly forty years.

Designer Andreas Langenbeck was involved in the G-Class project at the time and later recalled the challenges:

The G-Model range on the road.

We practically created the shape of the G-Class from scratch. At the time there were no comparable vehicles around which combined the character of a genuine off-road vehicle with the requirements of a safe and comfortable on-road vehicle. That was a challenge. We had to take into account formal considerations, but at the same time we sought to achieve a sympathetic aura.

New Style in the S-Class

In 1979 a new S-Class model came on to the market, with the internal designation W126. This was the first production model of the Bruno Sacco era and revealed the clear ecological considerations applied by Mercedes-Benz to both technology and design. The new S-Class had lost weight and sported a body revealing the latest developments in aerodynamics, but it had also become safer. It had a moderate wedge shape, integrated bumpers and narrower rear-end taper, which appeared unusual at first but was subsequently adopted not only by other Mercedes-Benz models but also by other manufacturers.

The initial styling of the new S-Class included ribbed side boards, which had the optical effect of lengthening and structuring the car body. These subsequently disappeared when the car underwent a facelift.

Mercedes designer Hans-Dieter Futschik described the styling as follows:

With the W126, design acquired a strong objective character – no more double chrome bumpers, and

The Generation One 126.

The Generation Two 126.

barely any bright-work, decoration or trim. The W126 seemed almost sober. The car's plastic components, such as the side boards (also known as 'Sacco boards') and the plastic bumpers were heavily criticized; technologically they were a significant improvement on the conventional primitive chrome bumpers however people wanted something to polish on Sundays and plastic did not meet their ideas of high quality.

It was clear however that the W126 had very beautiful and balanced proportions. These revealed the status of an S-Class without coming across as ponderous. The design was the right mix of volume presence and agility, it had static as well as dynamic qualities and the front end revealed the classic Mercedes image.

The 'Baby Benz'

In 1982 Mercedes-Benz unveiled for the first time the 190, the small Mercedes. It would prove to be the most important model innovation of the 1980s. Officially known as the Mercedes-Benz 190, and referred to as the 'Baby Benz', the saloon had no direct predecessors, so it offered the ideal opportunity for a new stylistic departure for the brand. However, there was to be no abrupt design break with other models. The bodywork of the new small Mercedes would incorporate the same traditional strengths of the Mercedes-Benz brand – quality, status, safety and advanced technology – as the models from the higher classes. Nevertheless, everything had to be reduced in scale. In order to appeal to new buyers, the design had to integrate more youthful stylistic elements without alienating traditional customers.

The result of this stylistic challenge was a compact saloon with a moderate wedge shape, clear but fine light-catching contours, distinctive C-pillars and a high, folded luggage compartment. Although its fresh, very straight-lined design had clear Mercedes DNA, it caught the eye with its youthful freshness. It was exactly what the designers wanted – the idea was that the new baby would become a talking point, and be seen as more than simply another Mercedes-Benz model. According to Bruno Sacco, 'The Mercedes 190 was a car designed to provoke debate in design terms. We wanted to attract new customers and therefore had to arouse atten-

W201 'Baby Benz', described by the Neue Züricher Zeitung as 'a refreshingly, unconventionally designed modern car, which is expected to appeal above all to new, young customers'.

Early rendering of the W124.

tion – for example, with a rear-end design that was unusual for its day with very distinctive contours. When I look at this car today, I'm forced to say it is still a very beautiful car.'

The rear-end design of the Mercedes-Benz 190 was not just a stylistic topic, however. The talk was also of 'aesthetics from the wind tunnel'. The drag coefficient of 0.33 for the 190 was around 25 percent below the average for all passenger cars of the time. Just as clear and homogenous as the rear, however, was the design of the other body areas. The roof section, for example, with its distinctive fold at the rear to formally introduce the aerodynamically optimised slope of the roof. In this way the Mercedes-Benz 190 became a stylistic ground-breaker for all subsequent Mercedes models that appeared until the early 1990s. Other manufacturers also imitated the design of the 'Baby Benz'.

The fact that this car continues to cut an elegant figure on our roads more than thirty-five years after its premiere underlines the high quality of Mercedes design, and its longevity.

Auto, motor und sport magazine observed public reaction to the newcomer:

> *By comparison, no other automobile is the focus of such interest, no other car currently arouses such interest in people than this new development from the world's oldest car factory. The body of the W201 encompasses the driver like a well-fitting suit, exuding the message that life can be comfortable even when the proportions are smaller.*

Looking at the 190 from the current perspective, Mercedes-Benz designer Hans-Dieter Futschik is effusive in his praise: 'This is a fantastic car, whose key visual cues are its incredibly harmonious proportions. It is light and agile in appearance and remains youthful-looking even today. This effect is created by the distinctive glazing, which makes the bodywork below seem youthfully light and gives the car a truly agile appearance at first sight.'

The New E-Class

In 1984 Mercedes-Benz presented the W124, which would later become the first model to officially carry the designation E-Class. The design concept of the new intermediate class was seen as the logical continuation of the 190 series, with more rounded lines. The fundamental features were defined by aerodynamic qualities, which were reflected in the shape. It was a vehicle that was both contemporary in appearance and subtly elegant.

The rear end of the vehicle was the subject of much discussion. Its almost V-shaped boot lid was a new and unusual solution that enabled the designers, despite the more aerodynamically effective high spoiler lip, to achieve a low boot sill (as always, form followed function). It also allowed them to accommodate the taillights into the basic body. While the clean, logical lines fascinated some observers, among others there was a certain level of incomprehension and

LEFT: **Clay model of the W124.**

The simple, straight, uncluttered look of the W124.

rejection. Ultimately, however, the solution developed by the Mercedes-Benz designers was taken up by many other automotive manufacturers.

Mercedes-Benz designer Hans-Dieter Futschik recalls the impact of the new E-Class at the time:

> The W124 follows the same design principles as the 190, but appears more grown up. The slanting cut-

out for the rear boot lid caused a sensation. There was a certain impishness to the lowered boot lip and rounded edges at the rear. But this design feature set a precedent, in part because it facilitated a simple sealing concept. Moreover, this E-Class had very straight lines, both horizontally and vertically.

The SL: A Sculpture

Athletic and sporty were the key words when the new edition of the SL Roadster, the R129, was introduced, in 1989. It was not the time for exotic design – not that Mercedes-Benz had ever specifically aimed for that. Rather, the objective was to present an SL that inspired emotion, yet at the same time expressed taste and style. It followed in the tradition of its successful predecessors, but nevertheless revealed an entirely new vehicle design.

This SL model, which boasted a distinctive wedge shape, was characterized by perfect proportions and sporty detail. The elongated bonnet sloping towards the road, the short, squat roof structure, the compact rear and the gentle, flowing aerodynamics of the side perspective – all these elements displayed clearly the Roadster's dynamic qualities and created a dormant powerpack of stylistic longevity. Particularly characteristic of its athletic appearance was the line from the headlamps over the wings to the upper end of the A-pillar. This turned the A-pillars into a stylistically masterful continuation of the front wheel housings. Moreover, with the A-pillar steeply canted, the design made fully apparent the concentration of energy expected of a Mercedes sports car.

The exterior of the SL was inspired. The former Formula One world champion Juan Manuel Fangio was one driver who had a positive reaction at the time: 'For me the new Mercedes-Benz SL combines at the highest level the features of a sports car with the qualities of a comfortable roadster and in so doing offers unique proof of the current status of automotive technology.'

This SL Roadster is rightly regarded today as an automotive sculpture. For Bruno Sacco, the R129 was 'pretty much the most perfect car I have ever designed – one identifies in it certain, clear professionalism.'

SL R129 with hard top, stylishly wedge-shaped.

The SL R129 in full convertible mode was sleek and beautiful.

An S-Class without flourishes

In 1991 Mercedes-Benz abandoned traditional decorative elements in the S-Class. The cleanly defined, unfussy surfaces of the top-of-the-range model (W140 series) exuded not only a sense of the contemporary, but also an air of superiority and reliability.

For Bruno Sacco, this model series represented 'a car that was almost purist'. 'At some point, size had become a stumbling block – nevertheless the car is very purist in terms of the way it handles surfaces and details. Little attention was paid at the time to the fact that we had removed the car's showy radiator grille – a modification we had been seeking for a long time but which had never been accepted internally.'

Unfussy elegance from the W140.

A new front-end design, with a full-surround radiator grille integrated into the bonnet and a three-pointed star on top, reflected the innovative application of traditional Mercedes-Benz design elements.

The rear end of the W140 with slanting taillights was idiosyncratic and at the same time showed a design relationship with the parallel W124 and W201 series.

INTRODUCING BRUNO SACCO

Tradition Versus Innovation

By the 1970s, making a curved car was no longer a novel idea and had largely gone out of fashion among US manufacturers. The streamlined cars of the 1930s had been designed to minimize wind resistance, but the flowing look was beginning to look tired, and buyers were turning to more boxy models with sharper lines.

There were new attitudes to size, too. In an attempt to compete with foreign manufacturers, European carmakers started to introduce 'ultra-compact' cars. They may have been cheap, but they also proved to be unreliable, which led to more legislation. The usual five-year, 50,000-mile guarantees were replaced by one-year 12,000-mile warranties, and insurance companies began to lobby government for better protection bumpers, to prevent costly damage created at under 5mph.

Perhaps the most significant socio-political events of the 1970s were the oil crises that occurred in Europe and America. These underscored the need to create vehicles that balanced performance with fuel economy. Increased pollution control legislation also began to affect sales of large cars with big engines, which had to give way to smaller, boxy, utilitarian, hatched cars. The sportier fuel-guzzlers were being replaced by what quickly became referred to as the 'compact wedge'. Although most car buyers were shifting their attention to smaller, more reliable, high-mileage foreign import cars, Mercedes-Benz was slow to follow this trend, thinking that a panic solution of downsizing would result in 'cramped, catastrophic cars with neither grace nor style'. Perhaps they were blinded by their own longstanding record of success or by the belief that a Mercedes buyer would always be a Mercedes buyer. Whatever the reason, seemingly ignoring the sweeping changes that were taking place in the global automobile market meant that they began to lose customers.

The AMG Pacer so disliked by all at Mercedes.

'Free sketches' of a 'world-car' by Bruno Sacco.

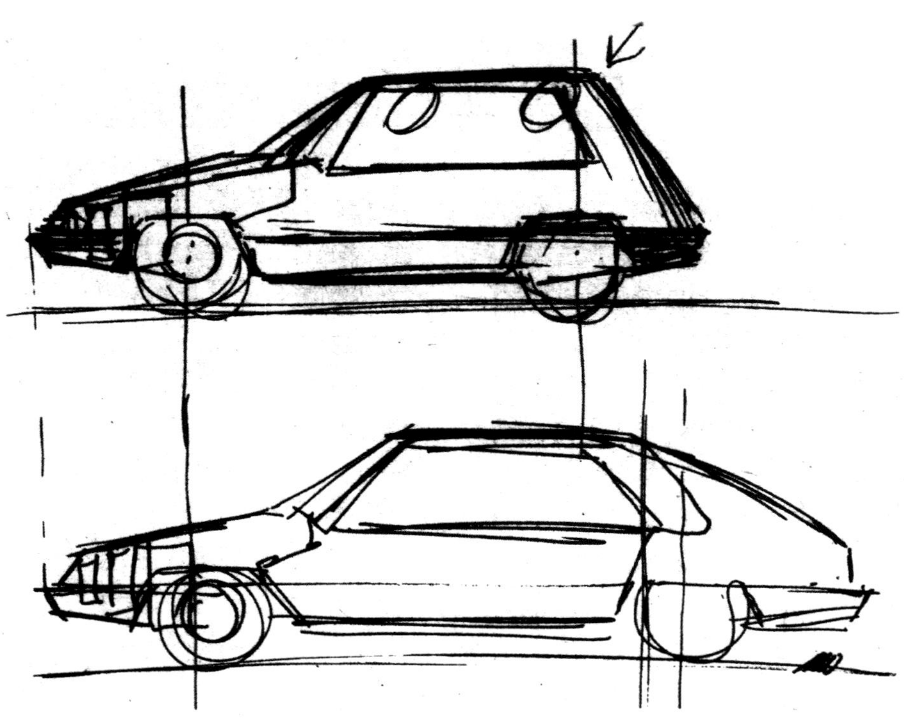

William L. Mitchell, design director at General Motors, was unrepentant in violating the unwritten rule of not publicly deriding a competitor. He expressed doubt that the Stuttgart styling department was even active in any way: 'I would really like to know what's going on there all day long. Their designers must be calcified or lazybones.' He later referred to their designs as 'downright ridiculous' and 'totally antiquated', accusing them of 'arrogance and [a] "We know what's best" attitude'.

Karl Wilfert, the head of the styling department, dismissed this as mere envy, as the SL was doing tremendously well in the US market. However, chief designer at the time, Hans Scherenberg retaliated with the assertion that 'real elegance means staying behind the fashion in the long run'.

After meeting Bruno Sacco at the Turin Auto salon in 1976, William Mitchell started to back down verbally, as reported in *Der Spiegel* newspaper:

I met the new Mercedes chief stylist Bruno Sacco, of which I was very pleased. For the first time, a Mercedes designer faced the press and explained the importance of a good design. I look forward to meeting him again at the upcoming Geneva Motor Show. Maybe my wish for Mercedes to regain its leading position in the field of styling will soon come true. Under his tenure Mercedes-Benz will include a small car in its line-up in the not distant future but a Sacco designed vision not that based on the knee-jerk reference that is the VW Golf/Polo or the US AMC Gremlin and Pacer.

Bruno Sacco was firm in his belief in the company. When pushed on the question of whether they were arrogantly ignoring the current trend, he was adamant that they did not need to 'blindly follow anyone's lead. ...Even since 1954, when we dropped the 170 model, we have always continued to consider a small car. ...Our 'world-car' will have a continuity of design of every Mercedes; we won't go submissively or blindly jogging down the same trail as everyone else.'

'Free sketch' of a people carrier by Bruno Sacco.

Early Years

Bruno Sacco was born in Udine on 12 November 1933 to Ottavio, a lieutenant of the Italian Alpine troops, and Margherita Martinz, who was of Austrian origin. When he was six, his father presented him with a beautiful 'Märklin' model, sparking a fascination for trains. His interest grew as he accompanied Ottavio on his work travels all over the Friuli area of Italy. Bruno would inspect every inch of the trains and carriages and began collecting train-related catalogues. What piqued his interest the most was the way in which these catalogues were presented, so perfectly detailed with drawings and specifications. He would set about copying the drawings and embellishing them with ideas of his own. Perhaps this was the first sign of a talent for design that was to come out later in life.

In 1940 Italy joined the war and Ottavio was drafted. Bruno and his mother returned to Tarvisio, the home of her parents. In 1942 Ottavio was captured at El-alamein and subsequently imprisoned in India for the rest of the war. Bruno lived in Udine and attended the Antonio Zanon technical college until 1951. He continued to draw anything he could, but less with an artistic eye than with an analytical one. One subject he returned to again and again was the clock tower near the hilltop castle in Udine's historic *piazza*,

Märklin model ranges that so appealed to the young Bruno Sacco.

whose bells rang multiple times every day. He admired its shape, its straight edges and the way it soared upwards as though reaching for the skies. To the young Bruno it epitomized his little village, which sat between the mountains and the sea in northern Italy. It was his appreciation of this beautiful piece of architecture that prompted his decision to pursue a diploma in surveying. He achieved the qualification faster than anyone had ever done before – but with little enthusiasm.

Early plate etchings encouraged young Bruno to draw his home town piazza.

Studebaker Commander Regal: early inspiration for Sacco.

Moving to Turin

In his late teens, Bruno Sacco would often travel to Turin with his father. On one such trip, they visited the Turin Motor Show. 'I was struck by lightning. It was my coup de grace,' he recalled later, with glassy eyes. 'I saw a stunning, electric blue Studebaker Commander Regal for the first time. I was in awe.' There was a second sighting a few months later of the very same car when the 18-year-old Sacco was cycling through Tarvisio: 'I nearly crashed the bike. It was "fate on wheels".' He knew from that moment that he wanted to be a car designer and that it would mean moving closer to Turin.

At the time, Turin was not only the centre of the Italian car-making industry but also the biggest international centre of vehicle design. Bertone, Ghia, Michelotti and Pininfarina were all located in the city, as well as manufacturers Fiat and Lancia. In 1952 the Sacco family moved to Turin and Bruno

ABOVE: **Abarth coupé prototype, 1952.**

Sergio Sartorelli at his desk.

While Sacco was working at Carrozzeria Ghia, the firm produced the beautiful, sleek Lancia Gilda. A rendering by Bruno in around 1957 shows a study of an aerodynamic coupé.

acquired an extra secondary school diploma so that he had the correct qualifications to enter the nearby Technical University of Engineering Science.

Bewitched and enchanted by the sheer array of designers in the locality, young Bruno soon established a rapport with various workshops. He knew that they would be looking for people like him once he had qualified from the university, so he invested in his future by giving his time free and getting involved with some of the styling firms. In 1955 he was awarded an internship by Carrozzeria Ghia, where he quickly learnt the art of model building. He was encouraged and helped by many designers, including Giovanni Savonuzzi and a young and ambitious Sergio Sartorelli, who both gave of their time generously to bring on the talented newcomer.

In 1957 Bruno Sacco made contact with Sergio Pininfarina, who saw something in this confident young man and gave him some work as a 'figurinist' (the official name of a car designer at the time). The quality and intensity of the work inspired Sacco very much, but it went deeper than that – he was starting to understand the importance of the role of a designer. It was an understanding that would be the basis of his belief at Daimler-Benz years later:

Creations are not always about the new and must not be 'art for art's sake'. In addition, each piece must have an in-depth sense of its own expressiveness. Being able to contribute to the evolution of a style is the most important thing to be able to do.

Bruno's 'freestyle' record car, 1957, and saloon.

While still in Turin, Sacco immersed himself in the car world, attending motor shows and developing an interest in sports car racing. Slowly but surely, an admiration for German culture emerged – the language, the motor racing (following Fangio's success with Mercedes-Benz in the Mille Miglia), and even the soccer, following Germany in their win against Hungary in the 1954 World Cup. (In those days, the Germans were the underdogs.) Most importantly, he was beginning to develop a passion for the work of Mercedes. For him, there was no greater car designer. He adored the W198 300 SL Roadster that had only just been released, but he did think that the saloon designs were a little boring. He was convinced that he could do better.

It was not until 1957 that Sacco had the opportunity to get a foot in the door of the German giant. He knew that they would be attending the Turin Motor Show and, ever enterprising, he took the initiative and made contact with the German consulate in Turin to request an audience with Karl Wilfert. He was able to introduce himself and secure a second interview at Sindelfingen, after which he was invited to join the Daimler bodywork department, headed by Wilfert himself. It was not an easy decision to leave Italy for Germany, and it troubled Bruno for some time to think that maybe he was letting down those in Italian design who had supported him. However, the pull was too strong and, on 13 January 1958, he began work in Germany for the princely sum of 650DM per month.

1957 Turin Motor Show.

Ghia stand at the Turin Motor Show: (left to right) Tom Tjaarda, Sergio Coggiola and Sergio Sartorelli. The man in the dark suit in the centre is Luigi Segre.

Sacco Joins Daimler

Sacco's first day at Daimler was something of a baptism of fire. His youthful arrogance faltered slightly as he began to experience the reality that bodywork design was not just about sitting down with a piece of paper on a drawing board. After a speedy introduction to everyone in the department, he was directed to a large drawing board marked *Masskonzeption*; he later learned that this was to be the W100 600 Limousine, but at the time there was nothing more than the chassis floor line, a steering wheel and an outline of an engine. Sacco's job was to analyse sizes and shapes of seat sizes, position and human body sizes.

Bruno Sacco settled in quickly, learning German by immersing himself in the culture, reading and carrying with him a dictionary everywhere he went. As he recalled later, 'I just didn't think it was correct to think in Italian and then translate it in my head to German, so I did everything I could to make my mind think in German.' His dedication paid off and he soon became a valuable member of the team, working alongside great men in Mercedes design, such as Béla Barényi, Karl Wilfert and Friedrich Geiger. He also met Annemarie, who would become the love of his life.

Sacco was not the only non-German working at Daimler-Benz at the time – Frenchman Paul Bracq had started there only a few months earlier. Over time, Sacco began to feel that playing second fiddle to Bracq was holding him back:

The style centre at Daimler was run by Friedrich Geiger. Draughtsmen and mechanical engineers worked side by side using preliminary sketches, 1:1 size sketches and full-size plaster casts.

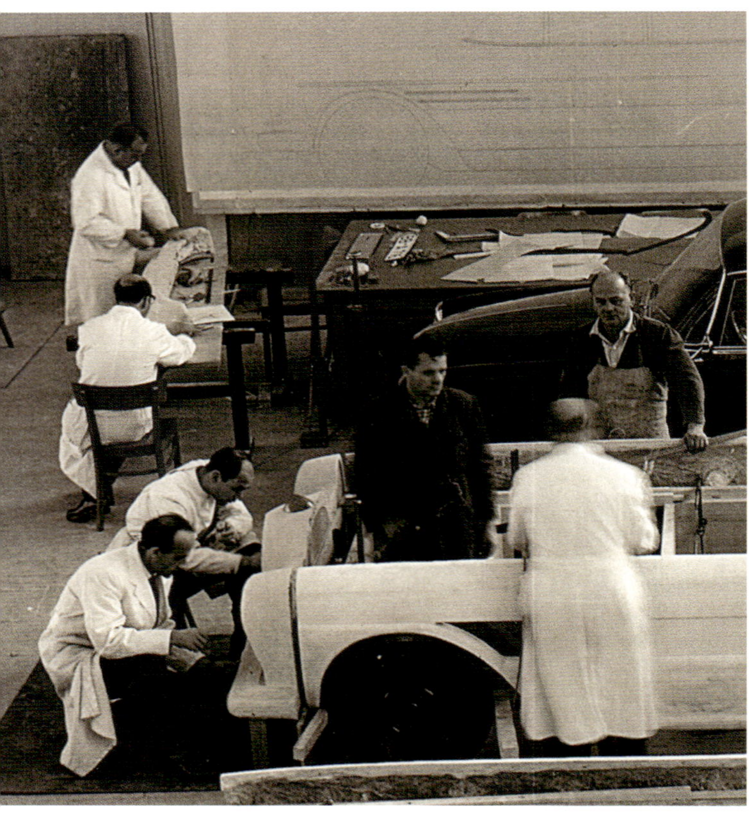

ABOVE: **Masskonzeption W100 600.**

RIGHT: **Bruno's beloved wife Annemarie with daughter Marina.**

Bracq was stylist number one and I was stylist number two and even though I worked on everything he had, I felt I could go nowhere without further development.

The difference between Bracq and Sacco was that the Italian had accepted that automotive design was heading in the direction of innovative engineering for safety. From this time, design was going to be about more than just artistic flourish. In 1963 Sacco made a big decision – he would leave the stylist division for a secondment alongside Béla Barényi in the safety department. He was well aware that changes were due in the industry, and that passive safety would play a huge part in the future of car design and innovative engineering. It was something that Paul Bracq seemed less inclined to come to terms with. It was an inspired move for Sacco, showing a strong commitment to a future with Mercedes-Benz.

According to Sacco, 'Béla Barényi was 'a truly great man'. 'He reminded me of a mad genius', he recalled later. The battles he entered into internally were testament to his passion for saving as many lives as possible.

THE EXPERIMENTAL SAFETY VEHICLE PROJECT

Things were changing in the stylist department. Late in 1967 Paul Bracq decided that he missed his home country, and moved on. Karl Wilfert went to Bruno Sacco and asked him to return to his original department, but this time as head of a new section called the Experimental Safety Vehicle (ESV) Project. Although Sacco had enjoyed working with Barényi, he did not need to be asked twice. It was also hinted that, now Paul Bracq was out of the picture, there was a possibility that, once Friedrich Geiger retired, he would be looking to him as possible successor. Sacco knew that he would have to start thinking like a project manager and not just as a designer.

Work soon began at the new ESV department on what was to become the famous C111 project.

The C111

(This project was originally designated as the C101. It became necessary to revise it to C111 due to complaints by Peugeot that the name might be confused with its range of vehicles.)

After a little over a year the ESV team had a working model and in September 1969 the first 'rolling test laboratory' was presented to the public at the International Motor Show (IAA), held in Frankfurt. It was a highly conspicuous affair, with an extreme wedge-shaped body, wing doors that opened vertically and, last but not least, a most unusual metallic orange colour, known as *weissherbst*. However, the technical innovations were not quite as obvious as they should have been for a test vehicle and for a few days it caused a buzz of excitement, with rumours that it might possibly be the replacement for the 300 SL Gullwing. The body

Early pencil rendering of the C111.

Early photo showing the gullwing door.

Front view of the C111 with the doors up.

consisted of glass-fibre reinforced plastic and was riveted and glued on to a steel framework; some technical features from racing cars had been applied to the wheel suspension and the car was powered by a three-rotor Wankel engine, which unleashed 280 bhp and reached a maximum speed of 270km/h, a remarkable feat at the time.

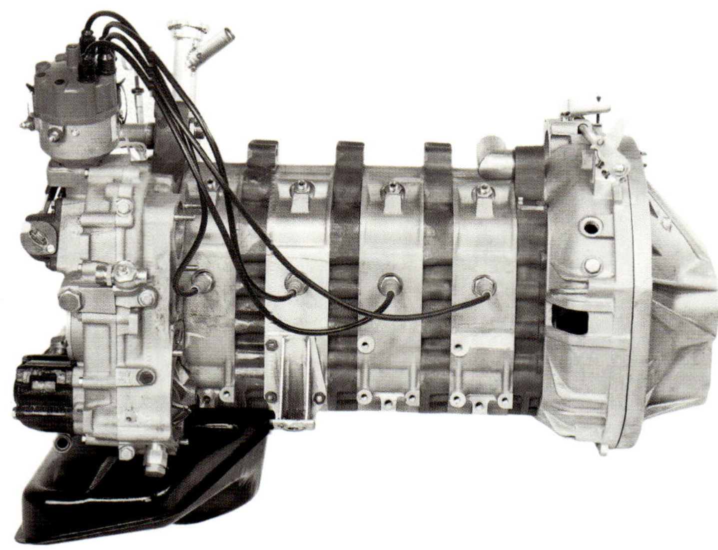

CLOCKWISE, FROM LEFT:
Early 'brainstorming' on the CIII.

The second version of the Wankel engine fitted to the CIII.

The rear view of the CIII/2 (right) was slightly more aesthetically pleasing than the first (left).

The C111-II

The success of the C111 and the modified C 111-II for Nardo spurred the developers on to new heights. But it wasn't enough: they wanted to break the 300km/h barrier. For this to happen, the engineers knew that they had to transform the road-going version of the C111 series into a 'proper' racing car. Only six months later, in March 1970, a significantly revised version of the experimental car was presented at the Geneva Motor Show. The C111-II had significantly improved bodywork, which afforded better vision for the driver as well as increased aerodynamic efficiency, with a Cd (drag coefficient) of 0.325. It also had a roomier baggage compartment.

Improvements had also been made to the engine. The C111-II had a four-rotor Wankel unit with an output of 258kW/350 bhp, fitted on a sheet-steel chassis and covered by a fibreglass and reinforced plastic body. This made it possible for the car to go from 0 to 100km/h (0–62mph) in 4.8 seconds and achieve a top speed of 300km/h (186mph). Modifications such as a new variable intake system increased torque up to 540Nm. The four-rotor engine was equipped with a single ignition and direct injection. The total kerb

Geneva Motor Show crowds.

The orange-coloured C111.

weight was 1240kg (2734lb). Other characteristics included a new configuration of the suspension, which allowed wider rims, a leather interior and the first anti-lock braking system.

Although there were many order requests and even blank cheques for the car at the factory in Untertürkheim, the C111 remained a purely experimental vehicle and never went into production. It became a favourite object for exhibitions at home and abroad and for a long time guaranteed a high level of publicity for the company. Even after the Wankel engine had more or less passed into oblivion, the C111 continued to bask in the public limelight several times.

The C111-II in the spray booth about to receive its new colour.

The C111-IID

In autumn 1973, a boycott of the oil-producing countries brought about an oil crisis, leading to a demand for new engines that, more than anything else, would use the expensive fuel sparingly. The most obvious proposition was the low-consumption diesel engine but the compression-ignition unit was still thought to be sluggish and noisy. There had certainly been examples in automotive history that displayed these shortcomings, but the diesel engine had long since been developed into a refined power unit, perfectly capable of driving a sporty passenger car.

In 1976, Mercedes-Benz decided to disprove the old prejudice and fit the new C111, now named C111-IID, with a diesel engine. The unit chosen was the OM 617 LA, which delivered 80 bhp and powered the Mercedes-Benz W114/W115 240D 3.0 and, with some modifications, the W123 300D. Thanks to a Garret AiResearch turbocharger and an intercooler, the 3-litre, five-cylinder, naturally aspirated compression-ignition engine, fitted in the C111-IID, now developed 140kW (188 bhp/190PS) at 4400rpm and 373Nm/275lb ft of torque. A five-speed manual transmission with rear-wheel drive and experimental Michelin tyres on 15-inch rims helped the engine to put the power to the ground.

The slightly revised body style of the C111-II.

The diesel engine version of the CIII-II.

Breaking Records

With this powerful diesel engine under the bonnet of a spectacularly styled gullwing model, painted in bright orange, Mercedes-Benz was soon geared up for some record-breaking drives. In 12 June 1976, the CIII-IID reached spectacular speeds on the test track at Nardò near Lecce in Italy. In the course of 60 hours, four drivers established a total of sixteen world records, thirteen of which applied to diesel-engined

CIII-IID WORLD ABSOLUTE RECORDS

- 5,000 miles with an average speed of 252.540km/h (156.921mph);
- 10,000 kilometres with an average speed of 252.249km/h (15674 mph);
- 10,000 miles with an average speed of 251.798km/h (156.46mph).

Nardò test track 1976.

cars and three to any car, irrespective of engine type. During the tests, an average speed of 252km/h (152mph) was recorded. Mercedes-Benz had proved without doubt that a diesel car could also have the qualities of a sprinter. It was even more remarkable considering that it also averaged 19 litres per 100km (11.9mpg).

The success in Nardò of the CIII and of the sparsely modified CIII-II spurred the developers on to new heights. But it was not enough. They wanted to break the 300km/h barrier. For this to happen, the engineers knew that they had to transform the road-going version of the CIII into a 'proper' racing car.

In 1978 Sacco's department caught the world unawares with a third CIII project, a record-breaking diesel car that was aerodynamically inspired and featured sharp body lines.

Pit-stop refuelling at Nardò.

The CIII-III.

The **C111-IV.**

The first clay model,
stored away in a back
room for posterity.

In no previous brand design project had technical innovation and design creativity been so powerfully combined. Numerous design elements later found their way into new production models of the late 1970s and early 1980s. The precise edges and clean lines that ran parallel to the so-called flow line also heavily influenced the design of the future Mercedes-Benz 190.

The record cars of 1978 and 1979 no longer had much in common with the original C111 of Bruno Sacco and design passed under the direction of Professor Hans Scherenberg in Sindelfingen. Only the basic framework stayed the same. The new car had a wheelbase that had been extended by 100mm as well as a track width that had been reduced by 150mm and 100mm at the front and the rear respectively. The very long body – now painted in silver – was designed exclusively on the basis of aerodynamic principles.

Using information gleaned from the car's record drive in 1978, and with the aim of meeting the higher requirements of the next race, the front section of the C111-IV's body was revised and fitted with two tailfins and front and rear spoilers. Four international and world records and one absolute circuit world record were achieved with the C111-IV, although this was never officially recognized. The modifications had clearly been very successful.

As experimental vehicles, the C111 series certainly did their job, with much of the engineering passing to the models that followed. For example, the front axle of the C111 was taken and put into production on the Mercedes-Benz S-Class W116 model, and the multi-link rear axle was put into production in 1982 on Mercedes-Benz C-Class, W201. Significant advances were also made in aerodynamics on the back of the C111 project.

THE MERCEDES-BENZ EXPERIMENTAL SAFETY VEHICLES (ESFS)

Under the auspices of Bruno Sacco, Mercedes-Benz built over thirty experimental vehicles for research on future automotive safety systems. These prepared the ground for numerous innovations, including ABS, belt tensioners and belt force limiters, airbag and side impact protection. Some only reached series production maturity years later.

By the 1960s it had become impossible to ignore the negative aspect of mass motorization: more and more people were being killed on the roads. In 1968 the US Department of Transport began a programme for the development of Experimental Safety Vehicles (ESVs), and initiated the international Technical Conference on the Enhanced Safety of Vehicles. In 1970 the first requirements to be met by ESVs were defined. These included extremely high demands in frontal and rear-end impacts against a rigid barrier at 80km/h, and in side impact against a mast at 20km/h. The test vehicles also had to withstand minor accidents at 16km/h without lasting deformations at the front and rear. Because of a belief that American consumers would not accept having to put on and fasten a seat belt, automatic belt systems were envisaged, which would envelop the front occupants when the doors were closed.

The US government also issued an invitation to foreign countries to take part in the safety research. In 1970 this gave rise to the European Enhanced Vehicle Safety Committee (EEVC), which is still active today.

At Mercedes-Benz the challenge of designing ESVs was taken up with great enthusiasm. After all, the company already had a great track record in this respect. It was able to look back on more than twenty years of continual safety research and, as long ago as 1959, had come up with the fundamental basis for all future safety developments. This was the year when the safety body shell with impact energy-absorbing crumple zones at the front and rear, and a rigid passenger compartment between them, had entered series production at Daimler-Benz.

From spring 1971, the ESV project went full steam ahead in Mercedes-Benz's separate safety research department that had been founded at Sindelfingen in 1969. All in all, thirty-five vehicles were built and tested over the four following years. The first test took place on 12 March 1971 with a W114 from series production (the medium-class series at the time). The car was subjected to a frontal impact on a rigid wall at 80km/h, frontal and rear-end collisions, lateral collisions with masts and other vehicles, and drop tests from a height of 0.5 metres.

The development focus was not only on occupant protection during an accident by means of correspondingly improved vehicle structures and innovative restraint systems, however; the comprehensive approach to safety taken by Mercedes-Benz in the era of these experimental automobiles laid the foundation for current concepts such as driver-

The first ESF 03, based on a W114.

The second **ESF 05**, also based on the **W114**, with an **SL 107** front /8.

The third **ESF 13**.

fitness safety through seating comfort, climate control and non-intrusive vibration/noise characteristics.

Where perceptual safety is concerned, the ESF 13 featured pneumatic beam range control, a headlamp wash/wipe system, a taillight monitoring system in the cockpit, a rear wiper and a safety paint finish with a light colour and contrasting strips. External safety features for the protection of pedestrians and two-wheeled road users included foam-covered front and rear bumpers, rubber drainage channels and rounded door handles. Fire safety was also taken into account: the fuel tank was above the rear axle, well away from the exhaust system. The fuel pump was, if necessary during a collision, deactivated by a mechanism that depended on the engine oil pressure. A valve system prevented any spillage of fuel if the car stood at an unusual angle. The materials used in the interior were fire-retardant and a fire extinguisher was conveniently mounted on the lower front of the driver's seat.

Mercedes-Benz presented four ESFs to the public: ESF 5, ESF 13, ESF 22 and ESF 24.

ESF 5

Developed on the basis of the W114 (*Strich Acht*) series and presented at the 2nd International ESV Conference from 26 to 29 October 1971 in Sindelfingen.

- Designed for an impact speed of 80km/h.
- Five three-point seat belts, each with three force limiters, front seat belts self-fitting.
- Driver and front passenger airbag, also an airbag in each of the front-seat backrests for rear passengers on the outer seats. This increased the weight of the front seats to 63kg each (standard: 16kg).
- Extensive structural modifications in the front end and sides.
- Kerb weight: 2060kg (665kg more than standard).
- Overall length: 5340mm (655mm more than standard).
- Wheelbase increased by 100mm, so as to maintain spaciousness in the rear despite the larger seats.
- Front-end extension including hydraulic impact absorber: 370mm.
- Experimental V6 engine to gain deformation space at the front.
- Dashboard with impact-absorbing metal structure on the front passenger side.
- All relevant impact areas in the interior were padded with polyurethane foam, especially the doors, pillars and roof frame.
- Doors without quarterlights, power windows.
- Headlamp wipers, beam range control, parallel rear window wipers.
- Side marker lights, taillights with standstill relay and control function.
- Windscreen and rear window of laminated glass, bonded in place.
- Pedals with rounded-off lower section.
- ABS brakes.

ESF 13

Stylistically revised variant of the ESF 5, presented at the 3rd International ESV Conference from 30 May to 2 June 1972 in Washington (USA).

- Restraint systems and other features adopted from the ESF 5.
- Kerb weight: 2100kg (705kg more than standard).
- Overall length: 5235mm (550mm more than standard).
- Front-end extension incl. hydraulic impact absorber: 420mm.

The changes to the external dimensions were primarily the result of the redesigned front and rear ends. The bumpers were now designed to be underrun, while the deformation path remained the same. The front and rear were extended to reduce the bumper overhang to an acceptable level.

ESF 22

Based on the W116 series (1971 S-Class) and presented at the 4th International ESV Conference from 13 to 16 March 1973 in Kyoto (Japan).

- Designed for an impact speed of 65km/h.
- Four three-point belts, each with three force limiters and a belt tensioner.
- Driver: airbag instead of belt tensioners.
- Kerb weight: 2025kg (287kg more than standard).

The fourth ESF 22, based on the W116.

The fifth ESF 24, also based on the W116.

- Overall length: 5240mm (280mm more than standard).
- Front-end extension including hydraulic impact absorber: 245mm.
- ABS brakes.

ESF 24

Modified S-Class (W116) presented at the 5th International ESV Conference from 4 to 7 June 1974 in London (Great Britain).

- Restraint systems identical to ESF 22.
- Kerb weight: 1930kg (192kg more than standard).
- Overall length: 5225mm (265mm more than standard).
- Front-end extension including hydraulic impact absorber: 150mm.
- ABS brakes.

The foundations for the safety level of cars bearing the Mercedes star had been laid with the development of the ESF 24. The summary test report (1975) was clear about its importance: 'The ESF 24 can be regarded as the completion of the project, as this vehicle represents the best possible compromise between the original ESV requirements and our current series production cars.'

At Mercedes-Benz, safety was included in the development specifications for new cars as a matter of course decades before the ESV programme, and in rapid succession a number of ideas first realized as part of the ESF project went on to enter series production.

The milestones included:

- 1978: premiere of the ABS as an option for the S-Class.
- 1981: driver airbag and belt tensioners available in the S-Class.
- 1995: belt force limiters and side airbags enter series production of the E-Class.

The ESF 22 engine compartment.

RESEARCH CARS

'The love of invention never ends.' (Carl Benz)

A love of invention was already driving Carl Benz back in 1886 when he designed the Patent Motor Car. He researched and calculated, tinkered with and discarded ideas, until he had finally built a vehicle that, apart from the wheels, had little in common with its contemporaries. Everything else was original and different, with a touch of genius. This was the first automobile.

Bruno Sacco knew how important design concepts were, having gained valuable experience working for four years with Béla Barényi in the experimental and safety innovation department. Everything needed to be researched, even it seemed outlandish or bizarre. The success of Daimler-Benz was always driven by research and innovation. Its engineering was always ahead of its time, setting standards on a global scale. This is particularly true of the company's research cars, which were used to test new automotive concepts and were always fully operational. Many features were then promptly integrated into series production.

This practice of seeking innovation developing fascinating research vehicles at regular intervals was stepped up from 1969. The Wankel or rotary-piston engine in the C111 was the first to be tested and this was later followed by other drive systems. The C111 car was thus the forerunner of the research cars. Their history began in 1978 with the Auto 2000, the Mercedes-Benz stepping stone to in-depth basic research for new automobiles. It was followed by the NAFA, in 1981, and, more recently, by the F100, in 1991 (the 'F' standing for the German for 'research car'). Since then, research cars have been produced with almost infallible regularity; they serve not just to test single components, but often also to demonstrate an entirely new vehicle concept in the form of a ready-to-drive automobile incorporating many forward-looking technologies.

Apart from research cars, there are other types of vehicle that serve to develop new models. Test vehicles are close relatives of the research cars. Their purpose is to put new technologies from the research labs out on to the test track. Concept cars at Daimler-Benz are near-production, ready-to drive vehicle studies. They position a future vehicle model on the market. One example was the Study A of 1993, which incorporated several characteristics that could be seen in the subsequent A-Class. Concept cars are equipped with new technology that is already in production cars or soon to reach production standard.

Vehicle studies are feasibility studies that show new ideas in the form of a complete automobile. These, however, are not usually roadworthy. This category includes NAFA, a short-distance vehicle that originated a good twenty years ago. It had a short, high body and, as such, was a forerunner of the Mercedes-Benz A-Class and the smart city coupé.

Mercedes-Benz research cars are fully operational because their goal is to make new technology experiential, road-ready and, as far as performance is concerned, measurable. This approach fulfils the purpose of providing insights into the car of tomorrow. Each of these special automobiles follows a holistic concept. Single components are not being tested; instead, the entire vehicle springs from an original idea. Although the somewhat unusual solutions can sometimes lead to controversy, it is all part of the visionary brainwork behind the automobile of the future. The public reaction and debate can give market researchers important pointers as to what customers want and need. Since vehicles must meet customers' demands, designers, engineers and marketing experts use the information to jointly draw up the technical specifications for a new research car.

Each car is a reflection of a clear strategy; sometimes it stresses the technological competence of the company, sometimes ergonomics, sometimes driving safety. The designers and engineers then have their work cut out in order to comply with all the specifications that result from the visionary ideas.

Entirely new and unusual ideas need to be spawned. Original concepts are constantly reviewed for feasibility, which is where information technology and simulation tools come into their own. If the idea works on the screen, approval for made-to-measure manufacture is given. Practically every part of a research car is built to order, which is a costly procedure: electronic systems are drafted, the interior compartment is redesigned and set up, the bodywork is formed. It is not simply a question of setting up a technical product. Every vehicle feature reflects great attention to detail and the quest for the highest quality of workmanship. It takes some two years before a research car is ready to drive.

The Auto 2000.

Auto 2000

In the late 1970s the Federal German Ministry for Research and Technology launched the Auto 2000 project, in which several carmakers participated. Fuel consumption was not to exceed 11 litres per 100km (21.3mpg) for a vehicle with a kerb weight of up to 2150kg. It was a very ambitious target for the time. The maximum for vehicles weighing 1250 to 1700kg was 9.5 litres per 100km (24.7mpg).

In addition, the car was supposed to accommodate four occupants and provide a payload capacity of more than 400kg. Mercedes-Benz met the requirements with the Auto 2000, first presented to the public at the 1981 Frankfurt International Motor Show. It had an aerodynamically optimized body with a very low Cd (drag coefficient) of 0.28. As many as three different engine concepts were tested in this

Early renderings of the Auto 2000.

153

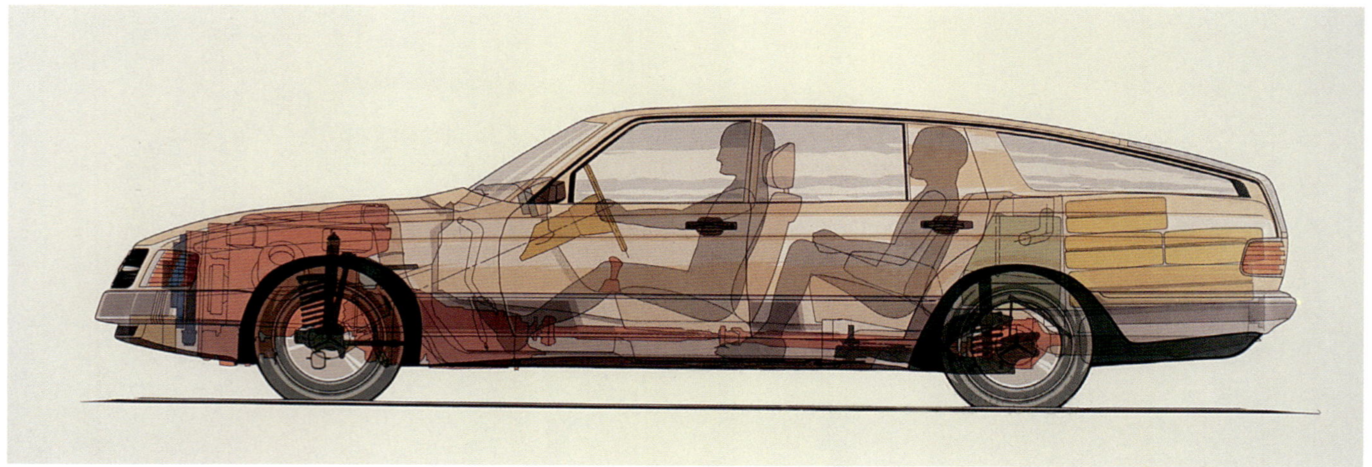

Auto 2000 Masskonzeption.

vehicle. An automatic cylinder cut-off system was premiered in a 3.8-litre V8 petrol engine. When only little power was required, four of the eight combustion chambers were temporarily shut down – today, this is a feature of several large-displacement petrol engines built by Mercedes-Benz. The 3.3-litre diesel engine tested in the Auto 2000 had exemplary accelerating power thanks to its six cylinders and two turbochargers; it offered an excellent range of 7.5 litres per 100km (about 31.3mpg) at a speed of 120km/h.

With the third drive unit of the Auto 2000, the engineers realized an ambitious project: the automotive gas turbine. It had several qualities, including low-pollutant combustion, low weight, compact dimensions, favourable torque characteristics, and the elimination of water cooling. All engines were harnessed to a four-speed automatic transmission. Integral seats for the driver and front passenger, with all the belt mounts on the seat itself, along with integral child restraint systems in the rear and pedestrian-friendly bumpers, were also tested in the Auto 2000.

NAFA

Congested streets, a lack of parking space, and long tailbacks raised new questions in motor vehicle research. Mercedes-Benz answered them in 1981 with a concept study labelled *Nahverkehrsfahrzeug*, or NAFA for short – the short-distance vehicle. With an overall length of 2.50 metres and an overall height and width of 1.50 metres, the innovative

City Mobil F100.

The **A93 city car design study.**

The A93 study alongside the A-Class, to show what became the A-Class family evolution.

two-seater contradicted everything the company had been known to stand for to date.

Its four-wheel steering even allowed the car to be parked forwards into tight spaces. Its turning circle was all of 5.7 metres. Even if the distance from other parked vehicles on each side was small, two sliding doors permitted convenient entry and exit. They opened forwards, and the side mirror folded in automatically. The car had front-wheel drive and an automatic transmission. Its equipment included air conditioning, power steering and seat-belt tensioners. The comparatively high seating position, low waistline and large glazed surfaces each contributed to superb all-round vision.

The NAFA study did not fall into oblivion. The insights it produced were incorporated into the design of the Mercedes-Benz A-Class, the prototype of which made its debut in 1996. In the Smart City Coupé, introduced in 1997, the concept of the compact urban car celebrated its coming of age. It has been manufactured in large numbers ever since.

F100

Daimler-Benz deliberately chose the North American International Auto Show in Detroit in 1991 – the first major trade show of the year – to present a very special automobile: the Mercedes-Benz F100. This research car gave tangible expression to the vision of engineers and market strategists for the automobile of the future. Never before had so many ideas and innovative technologies been realized in a fully operational car.

The F100 put the results of accident and social research resolutely into practice, so the driver was seated in the middle. Statistically, a car is occupied by 1.2 to 1.7 persons, driver included, so the driver deserves the safest place – the centre position, furthest from the main car body parts. Furthermore, the driver can always get out of the car on the offside. Passengers also benefit from the concept. The two seats behind the driver are offset, rather than fixed in a row, so that the passengers are a considerable distance from the dashboard, which likewise improves safety. Two

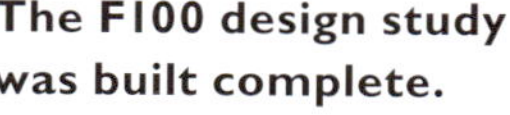

The F100 design study was built complete.

F100 rear end, showing signs of an evolving hatchback.

more passengers are seated towards the middle of the vehicle between the sturdy rear-wheel houses.

The body of the F100, with its prominent tail end, anticipated the customer demand of later years, when hatchbacks, estate cars and other vehicles with ample space became increasingly popular. The vehicle was unlocked with a chip card, instead of a key. It was inserted into a reading slot and electronically controlled and adjusted the seat and steering positions as required. Hinged and swivelling doors for the driver took away a bit of the vehicle floor and roof when opened. When closed, the doors overlapped at three points and fully compensated for the disadvantage of the slimline floor. Access for the rear-seat passengers was via space-saving, swivelling and sliding doors; the B-pillar was dispensed with to allow this, without impairing crashworthiness. The doors could be left slightly ajar and servomotors would then pull them into their locks.

On the dashboard, a central screen and gauges were arranged around the driver, with crucial information being easily accessible and a distinction being made between the log-

The main body of the F100 taking shape, showing the front door kinematic and the single-arm push out and slide rear-door mechanism.

Inside view of a rear-door assembly nearing completion.

ical priorities for safety, ranging from speedometer to warning. The F100 used a conventional cathode ray tube (these have long since been replaced by silicone-based displays in present-day cars). One forward-looking feature was the use of optical fibre instead of copper wires for signal transmission. The steering wheel had a fixed impact absorber and integral controls for activating the car phone and voice control.

Among the numerous electronic units assisting the driver and enhancing safety were the distance warning radar and the radar system monitoring traffic behind the car. This would warn the driver if there was a vehicle in the blind spot when changing lanes. It could also be used for automatic lane holding. When the driver put the car into reverse, a camera was extended from the rear spoiler, and images displayed on the monitor.

The compact front headlights used gas discharge lamps for the first time; known as xenon lamps, these are a common feature on cars today. The rear lights consisted of transparent prismatic rods, which served as light-wave conductors and took their energy from a central light source in the colour required for the immediate function. Together with the back window, they were cleaned by a rear wiper, discreetly concealed underneath the roof spoiler when not in use. The windscreen was cleaned by a linear wiper, which was guided across the entire width of the windscreen at top and bottom and thus swept almost the entire glazed area. A sensor in the windscreen ensured that the wiper was automatically switched on when it rained.

Also debuted on the F100 was the voice-controlled car phone. Solar cells integrated in the roof supported the batteries. Almost two square metres in area, they generated an output of 100 watts, which, among other things, provided power for the ventilation when the car is stationary, thus keeping the temperature inside at a pleasant level. By way of its car phone, including voice control, mobile fax and a personal computer, the F100 anticipated the communication and work options of later production vehicles.

Different engine concepts were examined in the F100, including a modified internal combustion unit operating on hydrogen. The vehicle had front-wheel drive – a novelty for Mercedes-Benz at the time – and rolled on CTS (Continental Tyre System) tyres with flat-running properties, with the tyre pressure being electronically monitored. The suspension featured hydropneumatic auxiliary spring elements, to enhance comfort and handling safety. The F100 also saw the first realization of the 'sandwich floor', a feature that subsequently made it to large-scale production in the Mercedes-Benz A-Class. In the event of a crash, the engine, guided by the sloped firewall, would slide downwards underneath the passengers, so that they would be protected.

General front view without cladding panels. A V6 2.5-litre engine is fitted.

With all its qualities, the Mercedes-Benz F100 was not simply a test mule for the engineers. Instead, it represented a new type of automobile. It anticipated the future of mobility, which has partly become reality since the car made its debut in 1991. At the same time, it emphasized the fact that the customer is the focus of technical progress when a research vehicle is designed.

Günter Hölzel, F100 chief engineer, demonstrating a cardboard flexible wheel cover made by Stephen Ferrada.

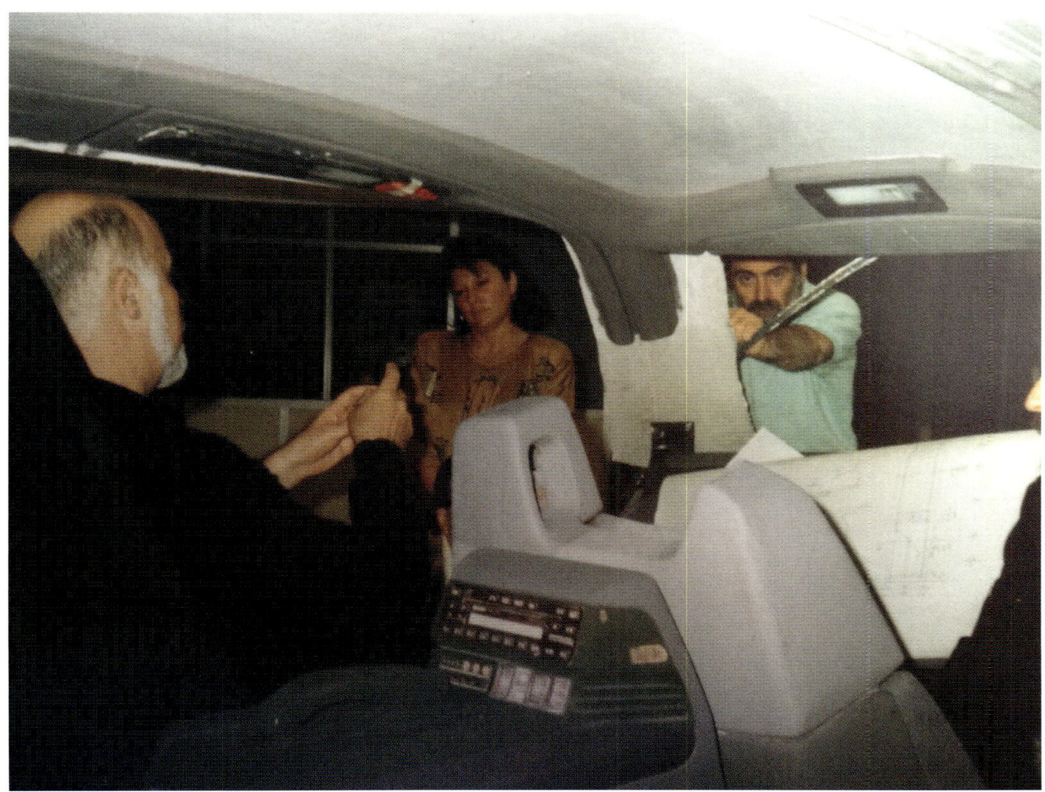

Bruno Sacco being briefed by Stephen Ferrada on the interior.

C112

For the 1990 racing season in Group C, Mercedes-Benz, in cooperation with the Swiss Sauber team, fielded the C112. It proved a great success, and the team was crowned world champion at the end of the season. The triumph was an inspiration for the Mercedes-Benz engineers. Looking for a way to test active dynamic handling systems for series-production cars, they came up with the high-performance C112 sports car. It was powered by a 6-litre V12 engine that generated 300kW (408 HP) and put 580Nm of torque on the crankshaft. The challenge was to stretch the physical limits while transferring the performance to the road and meeting the highest levels of active safety.

The C112 was the first car to feature active suspension, known as Active Body Control (ABC). In this system, each wheel was equipped with a combination of a spring and hydraulic servo cylinder. Sensors detected all the vehicle's motions – vertical displacement, roll and pitch – and eliminated unwanted motion by evaluating the data and controlling the active suspension elements accordingly. The result was an unprecedented level of stability in road-holding.

The C112 also featured active rear-wheel steering, to correct directional deviation, which can be caused, for example, by ruts and side wind or by road surfaces with changing tyre-to-road adhesion. Even in the case of a change in load distribution while cornering, the vehicle would maintain the handling and traction behaviour to which the driver was accustomed. An anti-lock braking system (ABS) and latest-generation acceleration skid control (ASR) complemented the technology.

Equipped with all these features, the C112 offered neutral handling, irrespective of load and roadway condition, even during high-speed cornering. Its safety reserves were thus higher than those of previous sports cars – a result that also benefited the series production.

The C112, inspired by the Group C race car.

The C112 was powered by a 6-litre V12.

ACTIVE AERODYNAMICS ON THE C112

The active aerodynamics were one of the highlights of the C112. The fully adjustable front spoiler and rear airfoil could be adapted to each particular driving situation, to ensure the optimum compromise between low air resistance and high down force.

During normal operation, the rear airfoil was inactive and formed an integral part of the rear body structure; in this inactive state, the car had the optimum Cd (drag coefficient), and lift forces tended toward zero. However, when taking a corner at high speed at the critical limit, appreciably larger wheel contact forces permitted decidedly greater lateral acceleration and more stable handling. In such a situation, the rear airfoil extended to the rear and upwards within a tenth of a second; in extreme instances, the angle of incidence was also changed. On changing height, the lip of the front spoiler would work together with the rear airfoil. The system allowed higher cornering forces and immediately extended the critical limits for the driver.

The rear spoiler was also used to improve the emergency stopping properties. With lightning speed, it was raised into the wind when required and helped slow the vehicle down. In addition, the brake system intelligently distributed the brake pressure between front and rear wheels to achieve optimum deceleration.

A super-car interior.

The C112 was also the first vehicle since the C111 to feature gullwing doors. Ever since the 1950s, these had been a symbol of Mercedes-Benz sports cars. The 300 SL Coupé (W194/198 series from 1952 and 1954 respectively) – a car whose excellent technical qualities made it stand out in its day – was the first to have them. The C112, with its streamlined body, followed suit.

Other components tested in the C112 were tyre pressure monitoring, which warned the driver of sudden pressure loss, a distance warning radar for vehicles in front, and some new sensor systems for the steering, clutch, brakes, doors, seat and mirror adjustment.

The gullwing doors returned, highlighting the C112's SL roots.

C112 from the rear, showing the raised gullwing-style doors.

FOUR CARS IN ONE. THE VARIO RESEARCH CAR

Variability was the design focus of Mercedes-Benz's Vario Research Car (VRC), a car that attracted great attention at its premiere at the 1995 Geneva Motor Show. Within just a few minutes, thanks to its variable body options, the VRC could be transformed into a different car. On weekdays it could be a saloon, but for longer journeys it offered the load capacity of an estate car. In the summer, its owner could take it for an open-top ride, while for heavy loads there was a pick-up option with an open cargo space.

The basis of the VRC was a compact two-door car, with a one-piece body that consisted of a roof, side walls and rear section. The body could be lifted off in a few simple operations and replaced by a particular variant. The concept was that the customer would not own the different bodies, but would drive up to a rental station and have a coffee while they waited for the service technicians to perform the operation. After around a quarter of an hour, the customer would be on the road again. The driver could decide how long to use a particular body variant, because the rental system would be just as flexible as the car itself.

The Vario Research Car was born out of research that predicted that people would have more leisure time in the future. The idea was that they would want a vehicle that was suitable for their various activities, as well as for everyday use. Owning a fleet of vehicles wou d clearly be uneconomical, so the VRC aimed to present a solution. It also showed the importance of a dialogue with the public when deve oping research vehicles. Mercedes-Benz asked drivers to state their opinions about each new concept, and in the case of the VRC, the feedback was particularly extensive and unusually diverse. The responses gave the designers many valuable suggestions for future production models.

This research car featured a number of futuristic technical solutions. The body change had to be easily accomplished and was possible only through the interaction of several components. The service technicians would place the roof structure on the chassis and electric motors would pull it into its final position, where special locking mechanisms held it at eight anchorage points. To release it, levers on the door pillars and the upper windscreen frame were activated. The servomotors then released the locks and raised the body slightly so that it could be lifted off easily.

The electric connections in the rear differed for each body, so there was a central terminal that automatically recognized the type. If, for example, an estate body was mounted, the rear-screer wiper/washer was supplied with current. For the saloon, the heated rear windscreen and lights for the boot had to be connected to the electric system, whereas for the convertible it was the electric drive for the soft-top that required energy.

One car for different activities.

The vision of the Vario Research Car was that the customer would not own the body, but would have it exchanged at a rental station, as appropriate.

The bodies were light and sturdy – the result of a new high-tech material called CFRP (carbon-fibre reinforced plastic), which was 25 per cent lighter than aluminium, but was exceptionally strong. Although they weighed only 30 to 50kg each, the bodies afforded a high level of stability and crashworthiness.

The Vario Research Car also served the purpose of further testing the front-wheel drive concept in a Mercedes-Benz – in this case in combination with a step-less automatic transmission – as well as active suspension (Active Body Control, or ABC), in the interests of enhanced handling safety and comfort.

The cockpit contained a colour display that was controlled by a rotary actuator installed on the centre console. It showed not only a rev counter, trip computer and trip odometer, but also route recommendations from the onboard navigation system. One special feature was the safety display in conjunction with a traffic sign evaluation system. If the official speed limit was observed, it showed a green circle. If the car was going faster or the correct distance from the vehicle in front was not maintained, the colour and shape of the symbol changed. The circle turned into a yellow ellipse or a red triangle, depending on whether the driver had exceeded the speed limit or the car had fallen below the safe distance. This function required the onboard electronics to be coupled with distance radar and traction control.

The upper part of the centre console accommodated a second display, which, among other things, showed information on the air conditioning settings and navigation system. Also, when the driver stopped to refuel, the system indicated whether the tyre pressure, engine oil, coolant and windscreen wash levels, and the lights were in order. Additional functions could not be selected while driving, so that the driver would not be distracted. Front passengers had unimpeded access, however, to all secondary information. The rotary control could sense whether the display was being touched by the right hand (the driver on a left-hand drive car) or the left hand (passenger).

The VRC was also the first research car from Mercedes-Benz featuring drive-by-wire technology, in which the steering and the brakes, for example, were activated electrically with no mechanical steering or braking. However, testing all this extra technology was not the main purpose of the VRC. It was body variability that was the principal concern. By way of this research car, Mercedes-Benz had underpinned its strengths, namely, the holistic design of new vehicles and the capacity to put them on wheels, ready to run.

F200

In the mid-1990s, the automotive world was asking the question, does the car of the future still have a steering wheel and foot-operated controls? The Mercedes-Benz F200 Imagina-

F200 design study.

The F200 was first presented at the 1996 Paris Motor Show.

tion, presented at the 1996 Paris Motor Show, systematically tested a new ergonomic concept.

The F200 Imagination was the product of the joint efforts of engineers and designers. The steering wheel had been replaced by side sticks – small joysticks in the doors and the centre console for steering and braking. Drive-by-wire technology meant that the signals were exclusively transmitted electronically to the relevant components. The conventional mechanical control elements used by the driver were now linked to electric and hydraulic actuators. When the driver pushed the side stick forwards, the F200 accelerated. If the lever was moved to the right or left, the vehicle steered to the right or left. If it was pulled back, the vehicle braked and, if desired, reversed after coming to a standstill. Should the driver need a break, the system could be switched to the front passenger's side stick.

Drive-by-wire is a technical solution that also allows the interior to be improved. If the steering wheel and the pedals are removed, the passengers have more space and thus more comfort. It also enhances safety because the cockpit and foot well can be designed completely differently.

The F200 Imagination embodied the systematic networking of electronic systems. One result was futuristic dynamic handling, with the electronics recognizing the driver's commands as requests for a certain driving mode – accelerate, brake, steer, reverse. The system could decide in a flash how to comply with the commands in the best and safest manner. In response to the actual situation, the computer would utilize the information from various sensors concerning travel, wheel and engine speed, road conditions and body movement. Based on the data, the computer would decide, for example, how sharply the wheels should be turned when cornering, or

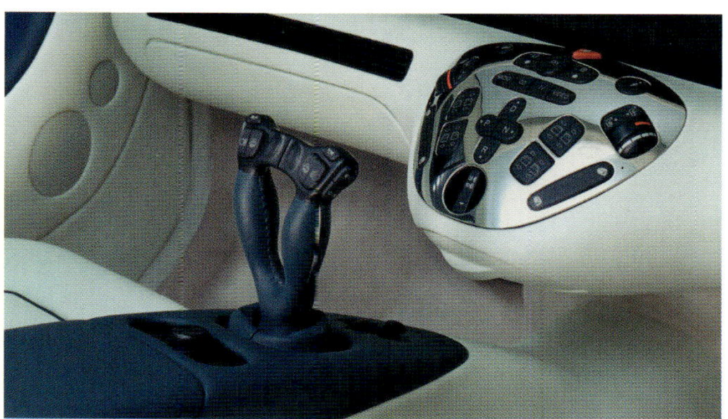

The drive-by-wire joystick in the F200.

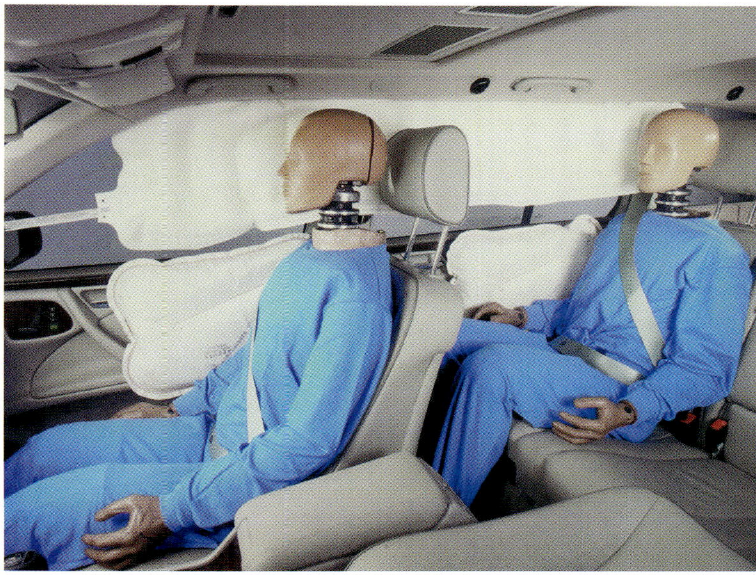

The first experimental side airbag curtain, later used in the W220 S-Class.

what engine speed would be appropriate for driving on a wet road. The system was interlinked with the active suspension Active Body Control, (ABC). Even in critical traffic situations, the electronics kept the car safely on course by intervening at lightning speed to regulate steering, braking, engine or transmission management and chassis control.

The driver can fully utilize the technical capabilities of the car without transgressing physical limits, which is a genuine advantage for safety. The electronically controlled rear spoiler system of the F200 also enhanced safety, setting itself upright in a flash and creating drag for better deceleration when an emergency braking situation was detected.

There was further innovative technology on the F200. The headlights, for example, featured variable light distribution. Six individual reflectors in each module, each with a separate bulb, were switched on and off depending on the situation and speed. This ensured optimum light without dazzling oncoming traffic. In bends, the light followed the wheel angle set by the driver, thus enhancing safety when driving at night. At high speeds on motorways, an additional spot reflector was switched on to improve the illumination of the roadway far ahead. The rear end sported a very compact light unit, incorporating nine separate functions: turn signal, rear light, rear fog lamp, brake light, reversing light, rear reflector, side reflector, side-marker light and ambient light. The unobtrusive indicator panel – a slender, arched neon tube – was distinguished by high luminous power and a long life.

Safety had been a long-standing priority for Mercedes-Benz, and this commitment was demonstrated in the F200 Imagination by the first-ever window airbag. It inflated across the side walls and considerably reduced the risk of head injuries in side crashes and rollovers. Since the vehicle did not have a steering wheel, the front airbags were incorporated in a kneepad underneath the dashboard.

Instead of the conventional rear-view mirrors, there was a video system with five permanent mini cameras. Four of them were discreetly concealed in the roof frame struts on each side of the car and, out on the road, they constantly monitored the areas alongside and behind the vehicle. The fifth camera was in the rear bumper and automatically switched on when the vehicle reversed. The images appeared on various monitors in the vehicle interior, where normally the mirrors would be located.

The F200 also had a transparent roof to flood the interior with light. At the push of a button, the electro-transparent glass could be darkened to avoid excessive heating of the interior. The glass had an intermediate layer in the form of a liquid crystal film of electrically conductive plastic. Electric current caused the crystals to arrange themselves so that the glass was transparent. This roof is a standard feature of the Maybach 62.

This large, advanced coupé was a truly pioneering research vehicle, which anticipated the major design features of, among others, the Mercedes-Benz CL (C215 series), which made its debut in 1999. The F200's electronics also prepared the ground for new concepts, playing an important role in future cars, including a special Mercedes-Benz SL in the R129 series. It was equipped with electronic steering and side sticks for test purposes in 1998 and was used for intensive trials.

Steering, braking and accelerating with side sticks requires the driver to think differently. It opens up new dimensions in driving dynamics, ride comfort and handling safety. The steering ratio and steering forces can be customized and adapted to specific situations – parking is different from negotiating a fast curve. To brake, the foot no longer has to move from the accelerator to the brake pedal, which enables the driver to respond more quickly.

The **F300 Life Jet** project.

F300 Life Jet

The aim of the three-wheeled F300 Life Jet was to combine the dynamics of a motorcycle with the safety and comfort of a car. A motorcyclist enjoys the freedom and agility of a motorcycle, leaning into bends, sensing the power of the engine, and feeling at one with the elements. The F300 Life Jet was designed to offer the same sort of unbridled pleasure of the road, along with the advantages of a car: even three wheels are more stable than two. The top could be closed, and seat belts were provided. The motoring experience could be shared with a second person inside the vehicle, and both would be unimpeded by protective clothing or helmet. There was no wind noise and air conditioning made for a comfortable temperature.

Never before had the world seen a three-wheeler that actually leant into bends. This was made possible by a complex electronic system known as Active Tilt Control (ATC), which computed the tilt angle and calculated the speed, acceleration, steering angle and yaw of the vehicle so that the tilt always complied with the actual driving situation. The electronic control commands were transmitted to a hydraulic cylinder on the front axle. Depending on the steering angle, it pressed one of the two spring struts outwards so that wheel and body adopted the tilt angle calculated by the computer. The maximum angle of inclination was 30 degrees.

Special tyres allowing large camber and slip angles were specially developed in cooperation with a tyre manufacturer. The rims of the F300 Life Jet were made of magnesium and tipped the scales at only about 75 per cent of the weight of a conventional aluminium motorcycle rim.

The **Active Tilt Control (ATC), governed by live action sensors, enabled correct road-holding at all times.**

The chassis of the two-seater was an aluminium construction weighing just 89kg, as long as a regular car, but not as wide, so that it could lean into bends. The bodywork styling resembled that of a jet. There was room for two people seated one behind the other. The special features of the body included an upward-opening, space-saving hinged door for the driver, a hinged door which swung to the rear for the passenger, and a fixed two-part roof made of aluminium and transparent plastic. In good weather, the two halves of the roof could be removed very quickly and stowed in a compartment aft of the rear wheel, thus converting the F300 Life Jet into an open roadster.

The lighting technology was in keeping with the unusual vehicle concept. The headlight had three reflector sections and two bulbs, and its electronics ensured the best possible roadway illumination, including in bends. They were linked to the Active Tilt Control computer and turned the headlight to conform to the body tilt; when required, they also cut in a special cornering light, which increased the range of the low-beam headlight by more than 80 per cent. A light sensor controlled the beam: the light came on automatically at dusk or when the vehicle enters a tunnel, for example. Neon lamps were used for the indicators, brake lights and marker lights, with the slender tubes being accommodated in the wings.

The engine – a 1.6-litre unit from the Mercedes-Benz A-Class – and the electro-hydraulic transmission (shift-by-wire) were installed in a space-saving position between the interior and the rear wheel. Power was transmitted via a toothed belt to the rear wheel. The 75kW (102 HP) output allowed acceleration from standstill to 100km/h in 7.7 seconds and a top speed of 211km/h. Consumption was around 5.3 litres per 100km (44.3mpg). To change gear, after stepping on the clutch, the gear lever situated on the right of the cockpit was moved lightly forwards and backwards, using the 'sequential gearshift' technique. It enabled particularly rapid gear changing and underscored the dynamic character of the F300 Life Jet.

The steering wheel, gauges, gear lever and seats of the F300 Life Jet all gave the driver the impression of sitting in an aeroplane cockpit. The segmented steering wheel was also an active element of the 'control centre'. Buttons for operating the car radio and phone were integrated in the side sections of its impact surface, so that the driver did not have to remove hands from the steering wheel.

The F300 Life Jet was the first research vehicle to be designed entirely on the computer and then brought to life. It thus served not only as a proving model for new vehicle equipment, but also to test a design tool called CASCaDE (Computer Aided Simulation of Car, Driver and Environment), developed by Daimler-Benz. From a very early stage, the computer was able to deliver data on the F300 Life Jet's handling by means of simulation. It was a fine example of the company's consistently unconventional approach to developing both the automobile and mobility. The F300 may have been capable of establishing a new type of vehicle, fulfilling the modern desire for the fresh-air feel of a convertible, the individuality of a roadster, the performance of a sports car, the comfort of a compact car, and the safety of a Mercedes-Benz – but it remained a concept.

SETTING TRENDS, NOT FOLLOWING THEM

Innovative technology becomes visible only when combined with equally innovative design. (Bruno Sacco)

When designing a new car, it is not sufficient simply to serve up bundles of creative solutions in order to make a product appear innovative. What is required is strategic far-sightedness. The time spans in which designers are required to think are considerable and therefore involve a major risk: the unpredictability of the social, economic and political

BRUNO SACCO: CHIEF OF DESIGN (1975)

In 1974 Daimler-Benz acknowledged the talent and passion of Bruno Sacco and promoted him to chief engineer. Just a year later, he was further promoted, as chief of styling department, following the retirement of Friedrich Geiger. From that moment on, until 1999, every Mercedes vehicle design was forged with his ideas, passion, personality and tenacity:

When I started at new stylist department in Sindelfingen there were only two designers, myself and Paul Bracq. Then when I became design chief there were 130 of us working as a team, including fifteen engineers and countless model-makers. However, everything was a fight with the board. I saw my job was also to raise the profile of the design team; if we were understood we would more easily succeed in producing the best vehicles in the world….

In my younger days I declared that Mercedes saloon styles were boring. The time had come to modernize those monotonous cars and break all the rules….
I now understand what the Germans mean by 'nothing but the best'.

When designing a new car, creativity is not enough on its own. It has to be combined with long-term strategic thinking.

A Mercedes should always look like a Mercedes.

environment into which a new product will be released. In terms of the life cycle of the Mercedes-Benz passenger car, Bruno Sacco was clear about the degree of far-sightedness that was necessary. He worked on the basis of a three- to five-year development phase, an average production period of eight years and a service life of about twenty years. As a result, the design of a Mercedes-Benz had to remain up to date for thirty years. Considering that the form of a vehicle will be decided in the second year of this cycle, the importance of design to the success of a new Mercedes-Benz cannot be underestimated.

In order to safeguard success in the long term, Bruno Sacco developed a Mercedes-Benz design philosophy during the 1970s. A design 'family' was to be created, to which all passenger cars bearing the three-pointed star belonged. The first rule was that a Mercedes-Benz should be recognizable as part of this family by members of the public all over the world. Should a Mercedes-Benz undergo advanced development in a subsequent model generation, then the identity of the model series was to be safeguarded. Bruno Sacco referred to this as 'vertical affinity' and established it as the central pillar of the Mercedes-Benz design philosophy. It ensured that a predecessor model would not appear

outmoded, even after the presentation of a new model generation. The goal of this strategy was to retain the positive aura of a Mercedes-Benz on the roads for as long as possible.

The second main pillar of the Mercedes-Benz design philosophy was brand identity. This called for traditional design characteristics to be maintained, further developed and featured in all model series simultaneously. In this context the term Sacco used was 'horizontal homogeneity'. It found outward expression in, for example, the design of the radiator grille, headlamps and taillights. Although there were formal differences in detail between saloons, coupés and roadsters, the family likeness was obvious at first glance, even to the casual observer.

Brand creation is a core factor within the Mercedes-Benz design philosophy. Every person today can recognize a Mercedes-Benz but determining how the car's design shapes the brand calls for expert strategic far-sightedness. Mercedes-Benz sees the design invested in its products as a way of introducing concepts. Design is not an equipment feature, but an integral part of the car's personality. It expresses the character of the vehicle by creating an identity out of the interplay between technology and form, tradition and future. And, since design must be long-lasting, it avoids short-lived fads. In this way, design lends sustainable strength to the brand – specific knowledge about Mercedes-Benz – and the unique tradition of the brand that stretches back over a hundred years. Thanks to continuity over many decades, Mercedes-Benz design has been able to sharpen its focus on the innovation values of cars bearing the three-pointed star, as well as on their future orientation. In addition to technical and design functions, the customer also recognizes the symbolic power of a Mercedes-Benz. In this way, what forms in the public consciousness is a subjective image of the brand that provides the basis of a distinctive brand identity.

'Ugliness doesn't sell well,' according to Raymond Loewy, the French-born North American industrial designer. Working in the 1950s, he was well aware of the interaction between product, customer and brand identity. He was convinced that people revealed a lot about their personality through their choice of car. After all, few products are as public.

More than ever, people today see car travel as an experience. They live more intense and self-aware lives than ever before. They take enjoyment in life's pleasures – and in beautiful cars in particular. The fact that they enjoy exhibiting their Mercedes-Benz vehicles in public as an expression of their personal lifestyle speaks eloquently for the brand's high prestige value. And design is the chief factor responsible for the passion that awakens desirability.

The Mercedes-Benz design philosophy that was initiated by Bruno Sacco in the 1970s has today reached a degree of maturity that is unique among brand competitors. No other automotive brand walks the tightrope between innovation and brand tradition with such surefootedness, expertise and ambition. Proof of this can be found in a growing clientele that understands and respects Mercedes-Benz design.

The Mercedes-Benz brand has undergone historic changes over the course of its development: for over a decade it has no longer simply stood for vehicles from the upper segment. The product drive launched in the first half of the 1990s led to successful new concepts that tapped into entirely new target groups. The number of new models called for fresh forms of expression that shared a common goal, namely, that every model series and every product should possess all values that customers associate with a Mercedes-Benz. The most basic rule of Bruno Sacco's Mercedes-Benz design philosophy therefore acquired a particular relevance: 'A Mercedes-Benz will always look like a Mercedes-Benz.'

A watershed was reached in March 1993. The focus of the Mercedes-Benz stand at the Geneva Motor Show was not a new production model packed with technical innovations, but, for the first time, a design study. The public admired the coupé study, with its four oval headlamps, muscular sculpted wheel arches and highly dynamic radiator grille harmoniously integrated into the bonnet.

When the E-Class with the 'four-eyed face' from the W210 series went into production two years later, one thing was clear. It was not just the new saloon that was to be seen in a new light, but the entire Mercedes-Benz brand. The slogan asked the potential customer to 'See Mercedes with new eyes!' From now on the focus was no longer just on the value of a Mercedes-Benz product, but on its importance to the Mercedes-Benz brand. In the development of the E-Class, with its elliptical headlamps, Bruno Sacco recognized a unique opportunity to link together technical and formal innovation. This new design factor was successfully

Bruno Sacco and his 'Baby Benz' W201.

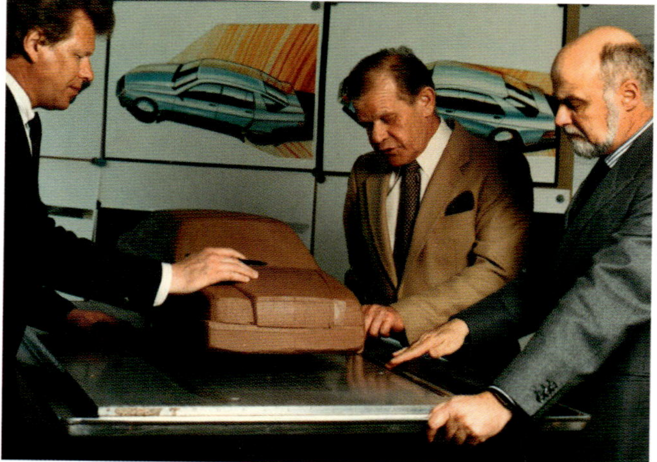

Clay models to follow form.

'See Mercedes with new eyes.'

Bringing design together as a theme.

replicated, for example, in successive model series, including the 208 (CLK-Class), 220 (S-Class) and 215 (CL-Class). From this point on, Mercedes-Benz approached competition in the automotive market as a competition between brands.

What preceded brand competition in the 1990s was a two-decade-long battle between manufacturers to create the best car image. This in turn derived from the competitive struggle to achieve best product quality. Nowadays, the spotlight focuses more on emotionally charged differentiation criteria such as brand image or design. The external appearance of a product is a crucial factor in a customer's decision to buy.

More than ever before, today's brilliant design ideas arise out of altered technological requirements. Knowledge gained from the wind tunnel, for example, calls for concrete formal solutions. On the other hand, innovative forms call for innovative technical solutions, such as the use of new materials. One goal pursued by Mercedes-Benz is to use painted metal rather than panelling, in order to make a not insignificant contribution to a car's environmental compatibility. As a result, today's design decision processes are always followed in collaboration with other development departments. Aesthetic authority, however, is non-negotiable.

ENGINEERING KNOW-HOW BECOMES DESIGN

In the early part of the twentieth century, the invention of pneumatic tyres, easily deformed steel, complex suspension systems and bigger engines sparked completely new auto-mobile designs. The saying 'form follows function', which was later much used, is a particularly apt description of the way in which technology exerted an influence over design during the infant years of the motor car. Mercedes was a trendsetter even back then.

For Bruno Sacco, the cornerstone of Mercedes-Benz design history is the Mercedes 35 HP, the first car to bear the name 'Mercedes' and a masterpiece of technical beauty. 'The concept was not only rigorously thought through in technical terms and stylistically unique,' explains Sacco, 'it was also extremely successful. It provided the foundations for a new era of automotive design.' The car, designed by Wilhelm Maybach and built as a racing and sports car, is also regarded as the very first modern automobile. Its innovation inspires fascination.

The 35 HP Mercedes was a masterpiece of technical know-how.

The pioneering design of the first Mercedes-Benz vehicle featured a lightweight, powerful front-mounted engine, a pressed-steel frame, a low centre of gravity, a wide track gauge and long wheelbase, a raked steering column and the high-performance honeycomb radiator grille, with its distinctive design. This innovative concept served numerous other manufacturers as the basis for new designs of their own.

The greatest challenge facing the development engineers at the world's oldest automotive manufacturer in the years before the Second World War was to marry technical innovation with aesthetic guidelines. An early example of their creativity was the Lightning Benz of 1909. Its design reflected aerodynamic principles and aesthetic calculation. The dominance of the Mercedes-Benz S, SS and SSK models on international race circuits between 1927 and 1932 broadcast Mercedes-Benz product and brand values all over the world. In as much as the victorious racers with their eye-catching design were reminiscent of the successful Mercedes 'Grand Prix racing cars' of 1914, these cars became the company's first ambassadors for continuous brand development. The Mercedes-Benz 500K and 540K models of 1935 and 1936 conveyed the message further still. Full of character, ostentatious in design and with flowing lines, they still pass today for objects of unsurpassed beauty.

In the years after the Second War, the Mercedes-Benz 300 SL gripped the automotive world. Designed as a competition vehicle by the ingenious racing engineer Rudolf Uhlenhaut, the two-seater was transformed by body designer Friedrich Geiger into an automotive masterpiece. The Mercedes-Benz 300 SL featured a space frame, which for structural reasons came up relatively high at the sides. This meant the door hinges had to be moved to the top, and the result was the birth of the gullwing door. It was also the first time a Mercedes-Benz road vehicle did not sport a vertical radiator grille, adopting instead an almost bestial air vent with a three-pointed star at its centre. The new front end came to define the design of all subsequent SL sports cars. Between 1954 and 1957, a total of 1,400 300 SL coupés were built. Production of the Mercedes-Benz 300 SL Roadster then started up almost immediately. Bruno Sacco was able to experience this at first hand. Having started at Mercedes-Benz in Untertürkheim in 1958, the young designer later recalled his first impressions: 'I was utterly fascinated by the way the body had been put together with such care and artistry.'

Bruno Sacco's own 300 SL, chassis number 0001.

A NEW ERA

The W201 190 'small Mercedes' opened a new and successful chapter for the Mercedes-Benz brand in late 1982. Until then, the brand had been connected solely with cars in the upper segments; now it served up the so-called compact class as a completely new vehicle category, positioned beneath the established Mercedes-Benz saloons. The new Sacco-designed four-door was designed to appeal to customers who were able to afford a car bearing the three-pointed star for the first time. Its attractions were not status-oriented style elements from the luxury market, but functional features.

Discussion focused on the new car's moderate wedge shape, which had clean edges, distinctive C-pillars and a high, rounded boot lid – features that later inspired many imitators. Attention was even drawn to the small crease in the roof area, which fulfilled an aerodynamic function.

A second masterpiece to receive critical acclaim in the new era was the Mercedes-Benz SL of 1989 (R129 series). Another new design, it embodied the dynamics of the roadster, with perfect proportions and sporting details. The

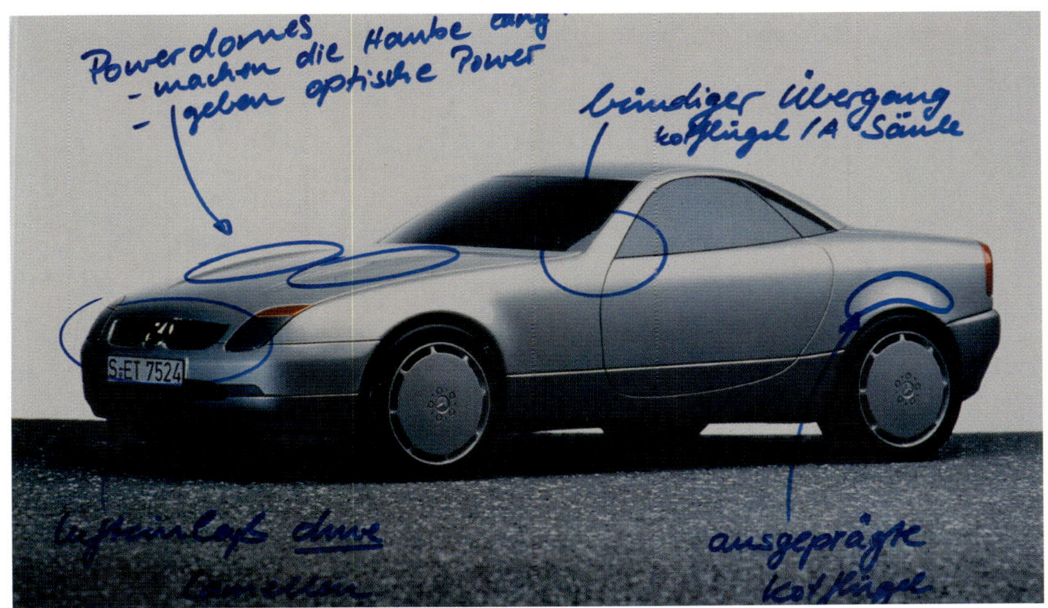

Original design ideas of
the SLK.

elongated, dipping bonnet, the A-pillars as a stylistic continuation of the front wheel arches, the muscular short hard top and the aerodynamic, gently flowing sidewalls collectively amounted to a controlled bundle of energy with looks that would remain youthful for years.

The Mercedes-Benz S-Class shaped the brand values of innovation, safety, comfort and status orientation like no other model series before it. The S-Class from the W140 series of 1991 waved goodbye to traditional decorative elements. Its clearly grouped, unfussy surfaces not only radiated contemporary style, but also superiority and reliability. Diagonally split rear lights underlined its innovative character, as did the new design of radiator grille. For the first time this had been integrated into the bonnet and completely encased in metal. The three-pointed star was no longer attached to the chrome trim, but sat instead on the bonnet. The S-Class had been transformed from a successful business saloon to a powerfully elegant trendsetter destined for the luxury market.

Having proved an immediate success, the Mercedes-Benz 190 was superseded in 1993 by the entirely new C-Class (W202). It was to be the last model series to adhere closely to the Mercedes-Benz design philosophy that had been introduced in 1980 and that, in comparison with other automotive brands, had been strictly followed. With its brand-specific, moderately updated front end, it was harmoniously integrated into the guidelines for 'vertical affinity' in the contemporary product range.

Fully aware of the growing complexity of what a Mercedes-Benz was to become in the future, Bruno Sacco knew it was time to relax the previous strict application of his design philosophy of 'vertical affinity' and 'horizontal homogeneity'. Differentiation of the radiator grilles was an attempt to achieve a simpler structure overall but at the same time, new vehicle-specific headlamp and wheel-arch packages were bundled together by the designers with a view to reinforcing the independence of a model series over all vehicles following family lines. This watershed moment was made public with the appearance of the E-Class from the W 210 series in 1995 using the so-called 'four-eyed face' design originally seen on the coupé study unveiled at the 1993 Geneva Motor Show. This original 1993 coupé study was eventually unveiled at Geneva in 1997 in the Mercedes-Benz CLK coupé (C 208). The product on model bore an uncannily strong resemblance to the Geneva concept, showing just how close to the 'finished article' the styling of Mercedes-Benz concept cars can be even well before they actually go into production.

A few sceptics at the time feared a reduction in the exclusivity of the Mercedes-Benz brand. What convinced them of the car's existential right was its strong individuality, its harmonious integration of pure driving pleasure and its elegant appearance, but also the easeful way the four-seater had been integrated into the Mercedes-Benz product family.

'We don't go in for quirky show cars with pointless special effects. Such cars may cause a stir briefly but they are usually forgotten within the space of a few motor shows,' is how Design Chief Bruno Sacco put it. Introduced the following year, the CLK convertible served to underline this goal further. Now the Mercedes-Benz CLK had established a separate series.

Design trends arise as a result of imagination and the courage to take risks. With the M-Class (W163), launched in

For the first time since the 1970s, colours came back into fashion in the 1990s.

early 1997, Mercedes-Benz dared to combine the elegance of a station wagon with the austere sportiness of an off-road vehicle. They succeeded in disguising high ground clearance, wheels in flared wheel arches and a raised seating position for passengers using a design language that drew to a significant degree on Mercedes-Benz saloons. The new Mercedes-Benz ML became a prestigious SUV (sport utility vehicle).

Bruno Sacco demanded just as much vertical affinity and horizontal homogeneity from the designers for the development of the Mercedes-Benz SLK (R170 series). Launched in 1996, the new roadster caused a sensation on the sports car market. It imitated the aesthetic qualities of its elder brother, the Mercedes-Benz SL and, with its power domes on the bonnet, even made reference to the stylistic features of the legendary 300 SL of 1954. Its stretched form and short overhangs front and rear seemed to symbolize the car's forward urgency. In terms of formal creativity, everyday practicality and functional reliability, the innovative folding roof set new standards in modern automotive design.

BRAND LOYALTY WITH INNOVATION

Bruno Sacco's theory that only the combination of bold innovation and brand-loyal design could lead to a trendsetting and durable product was confirmed – as it had been with the Mercedes-Benz compact class – with the arrival of the A-Class (W168), in 1996. The risks involved in designing this entirely innovative four-door vehicle, positioned below the C-Class, could only have been taken by a brand with the self-confidence of Mercedes-Benz. The new A-Class reflected innovative technology in avant-garde form. It was packed with detailed solutions that were pioneering – both stylistically and functionally.

The unusual ratio between the vehicle's length and its height permitted unique flexibility in the interior. The design of the front and rear sections reinforced the car's youthful aspect. The double under-floor was capable of accommodating a variety of different drive systems of the future. And above

Size design for the new **W168 A-Class**.

Rendering of the **A-Class** close to completion.

Clay model building of the **W168**.

Bruno Sacco's time with **Béla Barényi** is evident in this three-seat idea.

The sleek yet aggressive lines of the W220 S-Class.

W220 sketches.

and beyond the many practical individual features of the new A-Class, the car's overall appearance exuded warmth and charm. In the closing years of the millennium the A-Class was a testament to those who were responsible for the brand, who had the courage to steer a wholly new course in terms of technology and design. It actively relayed the message to the public that Mercedes-Benz stood at the dawn of a new age.

However, it was the S-Class saloon of 1998 (W220) that was to prove to be Bruno Sacco's great legacy. The brand's standard-bearer of innovation was a silky, elegant, well-trained athlete, whose traditional front section with integrated bumper turned it into a sculpture. The windscreen and rear screen were more slanting than had previously been the case and gave the saloon a lower, leaner appearance. Its muscular image added a new dimension to the internationally prized Mercedes charisma. Far from alienating through arrogance, the S-Class exuded confidence and individuality. It achieved a new quality of distinguished automotive self-assurance.

According to Bruno Sacco, design should balance innovative content with technical performance: 'Style and technology are equally important in car making… It is true we have become a model of style for all the others, it means we have done them right and done them well.'

For the first time in the early 1980s, Bruno Sacco exposed the horizontal/vertical affinity system used in the styling department to define every vehicle with a three-pointed star on the bonnet:

Because each of our models have stylistic similarities (horizontal affinity) and an evolutionary line con-

W220 sketches with headlight ideas.

W220 S-Class clay model.

sistent with the models of the previous generation (vertical affinity), this makes it immediately possible to easily recognize any new creation developed in Stuttgart… This upholds my deep-rooted belief that every Mercedes should look like a Mercedes and nothing else.

Following these ground rules, Mercedes has shaped its own destiny as well as its identity and has become one of the greatest manufacturers in the world. In the mid-1970s, when Sacco took charge of the stylist department, Daimler were selling 400,000 vehicles a year; by the mid-1980s, only ten years later, they were selling 600,000 vehicles per year. From that point on, the identity of Mercedes-Benz was shaped and would characterize the whole future production of the man-

ufacturer. In the 1980s Sacco also left an indelible mark on working methods at the 'Style Centre', encouraging designers to sketch their ideas first on paper in absolute freedom of expression.

Inevitably, there were always compromises that had to be made. Every product had to take into account the requirements of the production process, which was never ideal from neither a creative prospective nor a practical perspective. At Daimler, decision-making was up to a board of a few people, each one playing a specific role in the company, and Sacco would also have to seek collaboration with the technical board. Sometimes there was also a time constriction. He recalled later: 'I was forced into compromise on many occasions, something I hated… I was very upset when accused of being a 'compromiser' by a board member.'

THE MODELS

S-CLASS 126

The development of the 126 began in 1971, with feasibility studies. The decade was a time of significant change in the political and ecological climate, with two oil crises warning the world for the first time that fuel was not an infinite resource. Many scientists and studies were concluding that, by the year 2000, the crude-oil reserves of the earth would be close to exhaustion. The freedom to drive a car, which had become available to more people than ever before, might come to an end.

The new S-Class needed to be designed so that it could continue to be perceived as a luxury saloon, but would also be 'socially acceptable' and contemporary?

The 126 was the first Mercedes to be entirely designed under the direction of Bruno Sacco. He knew that this car would be a stepping stone for him to make his mark, not only on Daimler-Benz but also on the world. The W126 needed to develop further the already high standards of passive and active safety of the S-Class, as well as its quality and long-term stability. At the same time, the new type had to follow a completely different route in terms of weight reduction, environmental protection and aerodynamics, not only as a part of the history of Daimler-Benz but also as an example to the rest of the world.

During the period of the development of the 126, the whole automotive world was changing. As well as unprecedented regulations relating to active and passive safety, there were also, for the first time, restrictions on vehicle emissions.

The first aim was weight reduction, which had to be achieved without compromising the quality of build and finish that the customer had come to expect of a Mercedes. The targets were demanding:

• 50kg of high-strength steels for side members, tunnel and roof frames had to be reduced by at least 7kg.
• 28kg of light metal facilitated was to be reduced to almost half (15kg).
• All plastics had to be reduced by 5kg.
• The weight of the heating system had to be lowered from 43 to 38kg.
• The weight of the front seats needed to come down from 36 to 33kg.

The designers were certainly under pressure. There was a hope that intensive detail work on the body shell could lose as much as 50kg. As Guntram Huber, head of body development at the time, recalled: 'We even removed pieces of metal smaller than a fingernail.' They were helped by developments in the IBM computer, which enabled detailed strength calculations of body parts to be carried out, to optimize aerodynamics in shape, construction and stability.

High-strength steels were used for the first time in a production saloon. These special lighter alloys were 10 per cent thinner than the traditional materials, yet had to provide the same, if not an increased, strength in body stability. Today, knowledge of the lighter alloys is standard and applies in all car production.

The lion's share of the weight loss estimated by the Mercedes technicians, with values between 59 and 280kg, was achieved by the new light-alloy engines.

The final appearance of the W126 was adopted in 1976 by the styling department under the auspices of Bruno Sacco. After that, only basic detail improvements took place. It was important that the new type should be directly recognizable as the second incarnation of the S-class range, but also that it should not be as showy as its predecessors. In a comparison with those predecessors, the new W126 clearly fitted into the ancestral series and yet still illustrated remarkable technical and responsible progress.

ABOVE: **The world premiere of the new S-Class took place in September 1979 at the 48th International Motor Show (IAA) in Frankfurt.**

RIGHT: **Bruno Sacco was also responsible for the coupé's timelessly elegant lines. Here it is seen with a 1:5 model of the new big coupé.**

At the International Motor Show (IAA) in September 1981, the new Mercedes 380 SEC was the undisputed star. The C126 restarted the tradition of the great Mercedes coupés of the past. It mimicked the saloon design yet added the SL style grille for exclusivity.

'BABY BENZ' MERCEDES 190 (W201)

Bruno Sacco had already expressed his views by the early 1980s as to where the market was going, but he was adamant that design should remain at the forefront. It was the factor that could give a vehicle character and integrity, in a market place where mechanical performance could be rather similar. Despite classifications such as 'saloon', 'hatchback', 'estate' and 'people carrier', manufacturers could still be flexible in their market place. This idea was predomi-

The W201 'Baby Benz' fresh on the drawing board.

Free sketching ideas of shapes and profiles always took place. Nothing was taken for granted.

W201 clay modelling.

nant in the mind of chief designer Sacco when designing the W201, the model that granted access to a wider public and would become the turning point in the Mercedes-Benz as a company.

Recognizing the signs of the times, Mercedes-Benz wanted to launch a model that could transfer brand values such as safety and comfort from the higher-class vehicles to a compact segment, without compromises. The public and the press looked forward to 8 December 1982 with great expectations, when the compact-class saloons would be presented. The 190/190 E model broke records at the Nardò test track. Its success was surely in part due to its distinctive appearance: a clear wedge shape, fine light-catching edges, precise contours, and a striking tall rear. Sacco's design was initially deemed to be a formal-aesthetic provocation, but it prevailed. The eventual C-Class, as well as other luxury-class vehicles, would be inspired by the 'Baby Benz'.

The 190 models did not replace previous types, but completed the traditional Mercedes-Benz passenger car programme by a third main line. The new range of models was characterized by more compact measures, reduced weight and increased economy without making any compromises in terms of handling performance, safety and reliability. Energy consumption was minimized by using high-strength sheet steel and other weight-reducing materials, as well as by the imposition of aerodynamic optimization. Passive safety had been the reason for providing the series 126 with a forked beam in the front end. This design principle also featured on the compact-class vehicles, so that they fulfilled the criterion of an asymmetric head-on impact with 40 per cent overlapping at 55km/h. As a result, the 190 models were absolutely as safe as the big S-Class saloons.

Excellent handling was made possible by newly developed front and rear axle constructions. The damper strut front axle with individual A-arm suspension and anti-dive device guaranteed a good straight-running stability. Its low overall height created favourable conditions in the engine compartment. One revolutionary factor was the multi-link rear suspension, in which each rear wheel was led by an independent control arm. This optimal wheel control largely compensated for lateral and longitudinal forces in all driving conditions, thus preventing unwanted steering movements of the wheel.

W201 wind-tunnel testing and fine adjustments on clay bodywork.

IBM computer mapping for aerodynamic optimization.

Brand recognition and horizontal affinity in the model line of 123, 201 and 126.

The 190E W201 finished model.

Further advantages of this innovative construction were that it was low in weight and took up a small amount of space.

Bruno Sacco was clear about the importance of the 190 in the history of Mercedes-Benz:

> Apart from the 126 S-Class I believe the 201 is the ideal example of incorporating innovation into tradition… The 190 was the car that convinced people and the press that Mercedes could and was willing to change. Before the 190 the press would shout from the rooftops that every model was the same as what came before; it would drive me mad…After the 190… it stopped.

W/S/C124 RANGE

Sacco said the following about the 124 series:

> An essential message is that each model is part of a so-called 'family of forms'. The entire model series produced at any particular time must share a clearly definable and significant number of common formal elements. This…is what was called horizontal homogeneity. …and this is perceived by the public as 'corporate identity'…all the cars must show a steady progression from one model generation to the next. This way, we are also able to define a so-called vertical continuity.
>
> The outgoing model will not seem outdated the moment the new model is presented. On the contrary, it will maintain its qualities in the automotive 'landscape' for years. Experience has taught us that forms that are too fashionable and flamboyant are consumed more rapidly than those that purposely avoid special effects. Of course, any form tends to become outdated sooner or later and design can help accelerate this process. However, I believe that each and every Mercedes model has a certain potential to become a classic later.
>
> All Mercedes cars incorporate a series of prerogatives that are distinctive of their brand. As far as design is concerned, these are unmistakable but also symbolic stylistic elements: for example, we think the front section is the face of a car, one of its greatest expressive parts, epitomising the system of ideal and

Horizontal affinity through the W201, W124 and W126.

The W124 E-Class.

Clay model shape forming for the W124.

The 124 range was an evolutionary derivation of the 190 W201 series, although, as always, there was an added smoothness and finesse of line from the predecessor.

The coarseness of the 124's line shocked some customers but it was soon accepted as understated elegance.

material attributes and values commonly associated with our cars and our company.

Formal solutions being typical for Mercedes can also be found in other details: the tails of our cars have such functional characteristics that we have been able to continue developing the through all the latest series generation. In developing other details, we can also identify Mercedes' own formal grammar. The intersection of lines, the reflection of light created by surfaces, the dissipation of rays, the curvatures that create an absolutely unmistakable bonnet, for example: all this is not just the product of a designer's work, but also of our skilled model-makers...

At the turn of the year 1984/85 a new model generation appeared in the medium-size series. It became the successor of series 123 and was produced for nine years.

In 1984, the first E-Class offered unique diversity at a time when the Mercedes line was only just becoming available to a wider range of clients. The people of Stuttgart had come up with the title Mittleren Mercedes-Klasse (the 'Mercedes of the middle class') in the 1950s, to designate a market segment that would become so important to them. The car was neither too big nor too small; it was not too luxurious, but it was built with the same attention to detail as every other Mercedes. The series offered a model for everyone, from a taxi driver to a businessman who could not yet afford to own or drive a Sonderklasse vehicle.

W124 model testing in the mini wind tunnel, allowing for on-the-spot alterations.

In terms of style, the 124 shocked some conservative customers. Its high-boot corner profile and chrome-free bodywork, apart from the grille and three-spoke stars, confirmed the direction taken by the small saloon 190 that had been presented two years earlier. The value of the 124 was in its sober and refined lines, which made it a model of discreet elegance. The extra rake of the windscreen, headlights and grille was also a nod to what had been learned from the aerodynamics of the W201, and had the added benefit of improving fuel consumption.

A total of 2,058,777 saloons were produced between 1984 and 1995, to which were added 340,503 station wagons. The Mercedes W124 was the first series to offer such a combination of successful vehicle options; it also formed the basis of every E-Class descendant through to 2014.

SL-CLASS R129

With its classic proportions it was an automobile sculpture and the most perfect car of my career.
(Bruno Sacco)

The team of designers under Bruno Sacco were faced with a momentous challenge: just as the S-Class was the flagship of the saloon world, the SL was not only the flagship luxury sports car but also needed to echo the W198 SL Roadster of 1957 that everyone loved, including Bruno himself. The aim was simply to create a convertible that fitted in with the SL brief. It had to radiate style and elegance but it also, most importantly, had to 'spark emotion'.

R129 SL wind-tunnel testing with the top down.

R129 SL wind-tunnel testing with the top up.

The SL model was not exempt from Sacco's philosophy of horizontal and vertical affinity. It had to be recognizable as an evolution of past models but it also had to have an entirely new look and a modern character of its own:

We wanted to remove the aggression from the car, which I know doesn't sound very logical with a sports car.

The world premiere of the new 129 series SL in March 1989 was one of the main attractions of the Geneva Motor Show. The new types 300 SL, 300 SL-24 and 500 SL shared no common features with their preceding models except for their overall concept. As had been the case eighteen years before, when the 350 SL demonstrated many innovative construction details that were significant in terms of automotive progress, the 129 series SL was a completely new car.

The new SL generation convinced by a harmonic and very successful stylistic shape. It expressed not only a dynamism and sportiness, but also comfort and elegance. On the one hand, the design presented itself as traditional; on the other hand, its new solutions of many details looked far into the future.

A total of 204,940 cars were built between 1988 and 2001 (excluding AMG versions).

NEW S-CLASS 140

The S-Class of 1991 embodied the notion of functional modernity by waiving all redundant frills.

In March 1991 the new S-Class generation (designated internally as the 140 series) made its debut at the Geneva Motor Show. The body design incorporated the typical traditional Mercedes-Benz stylistic elements, enabling it to fit in seamlessly with the visual appearance of the company's other passenger cars. As had already been the case with the SL models in the 129 series, the trademark radiator grille of the new S-Class was given a new stylistic interpretation while retaining the traditional basic shape.

The variation on the classic theme was designated the 'integrated radiator'. With a much narrower chrome frame, the radiator shell was organically integrated into the engine cover and, for the first time, the Mercedes star was positioned not on top of the radiator grille, but slightly to the rear on the bonnet. The overall aim of the design concept of the new S-Class generation was to achieve a high degree of aerodynamic quality while at the same time ensuring maximum everyday practicality.

What I was originally aiming for was a shape that embodied aerodynamic efficiency, rather than out-

First design sketches of the new S-Class.

Working with clay modelling for various shapes of the W140.

BELOW: **For the first time the iconic radiator grille was inset. This image shows the various bucks, dated around 1985.**

right opulence. Yet over the years, that brief changed, with W140's sheer size eventually evolving into a statement of blunt superiority.

I still see it every day and think to myself 'that should have been 100mm lower in height', but, as was often the case, I was overruled by the engineering department. I was even 'semi-withdrawn' from 140 projects due to my objections.

The 140 turned out to be the last indiscriminately engineering-driven S-class model; the last of its kind for which money was no object. However, it was not just the engineering ethos that had changed in the aftermath of the 140's tumultuous launch; it is obvious that a shift of power took place at some point during the early 1990s, when Bruno Sacco's 'vertical affinity/horizontal homogeneity' design philosophy was overruled in favour of 'design freedom'. This approach eschewed the stringent, rational form language that Sacco had so painstakingly nurtured in favour of a trendier, much less profound approach.

At the Turin Motor Show in 1994, at the presentation of the SLK prototype, Bruno Sacco delivered a crucial speech on the philosophy of Mercedes car design, echoing the concepts he had been outlining since the very beginning of the 'style centre':

How do we conceive our company's designs today in the context of our history and current technical demands and possibilities? We must continue to follow the three basic principles.

1 A Mercedes must always look like a Mercedes.

2 It should symbolize all the values that are the hallmark of an authentic Mercedes and that our customers expect of it.

3 The design should include as much innovation as possible while at the same time remaining true to the values of the brand.

It is highly important that both the driver and the passengers have the clear sensation of being in a Mercedes once they are seated in any of our cars. This feeling is induced not only by the design but also by the finishing, the choice of materials, and even the tactile impact with interior surfaces. This way, it is not difficult for customers to establish a relationship of trust with the marque, especially in terms of reliability and continuity.

Bruno Sacco's team, though, soon had to get ready for a new venture. The time had come to meet one of the greatest challenges in Mercedes history: the A-Class, a smart front-wheel-drive passenger car. It would add a fifth class to the range of the Stuttgart-based company.

W168 A-CLASS

At the International Motor Show in Frankfurt in September 1993, Mercedes Benz presented the close-to-production study of a prospective new vehicle class with front-wheel drive. The 'Vision A 93' attracted instant worldwide attention, having emphatically demonstrated that it was possible to create a unique new vehicle concept that reconciled seemingly conflicting aims – although compact in size, the vehicle offered a large, adaptable interior and Mercedes Benz safety standards.

Despite an external length of just 3.35m, the generous amount of space on board and ease of access rivalled those of full-size mid-range saloons. The 'Vision A 93' was also extremely adaptable: from a comfortable four-seater to an estate with a load capacity of 1000 litres, every conceivable customer wish could be met. The basis for the revolutionary spatial concept was a new, raised floor assembly which – to some extent as a side effect – made possible a level of crash safety never before seen in a compact car.

The 'Vision A 93' was far more than just a design or technology study; it was designed to point the way ahead to a market segment at that point not yet defined by Mercedes Benz and influence the development of the future A-Class. Following an overwhelmingly positive response from the public and the media, the company pressed ahead with selecting the production site. On 4 December 1993, after long and difficult negotiations, Mercedes Benz decided that the new A Class would be produced in Rastatt, thereby favouring the third Mercedes Benz Passenger Car plant, inaugurated in 1992, over other locations that had been considered in France, the UK and the Czech Republic.

In 1994 Mercedes Benz exhibited the slightly modified concept vehicle at the Geneva Motor Show under the name 'Studie A'. The US publication Motor Week awarded it the title 'Best Concept Car 1994'.

As the development of the A-Class progressed, the press and the public were kept informed of all the latest details. It was an absolutely unique move in the history of the com-

The 'Vision A 93' was far more than just a design or technology study. The clay models show variations in size and shape.

pany, particularly so far in advance of the start of series production. In August 1994, sixty motoring journalists from Germany and other countries got to test drive the DM 1.5-million prototype and experience the practical strengths of the future A Class under normal driving conditions.

At the Frankfurt Motor Show in September 1995, two years after the world premiere of the 'Vision A 93', the company presented the interior concept of the A Class and announced that the new vehicle was to be 225mm longer than the study. This meant that the respectable amount of space already on offer, particularly in the load compartment, had been increased further still. The reaction to the extensive adaptability of the interior was very positive. At the same time, the company launched the 'Forum for the New Car', which aimed to provide a platform to give an interested public the latest information about the A Class.

The company also announced at the Frankfurt Motor Show that it intended to produce the new vehicle not only in Rastatt, but also in Brazil, where it aimed to expand production capacity. The go-ahead was given six months later

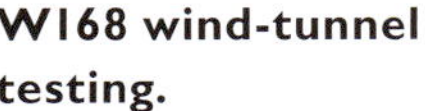

W168 wind-tunnel testing.

The frontal off-centre crash test proved that even smaller vehicles can be safe.

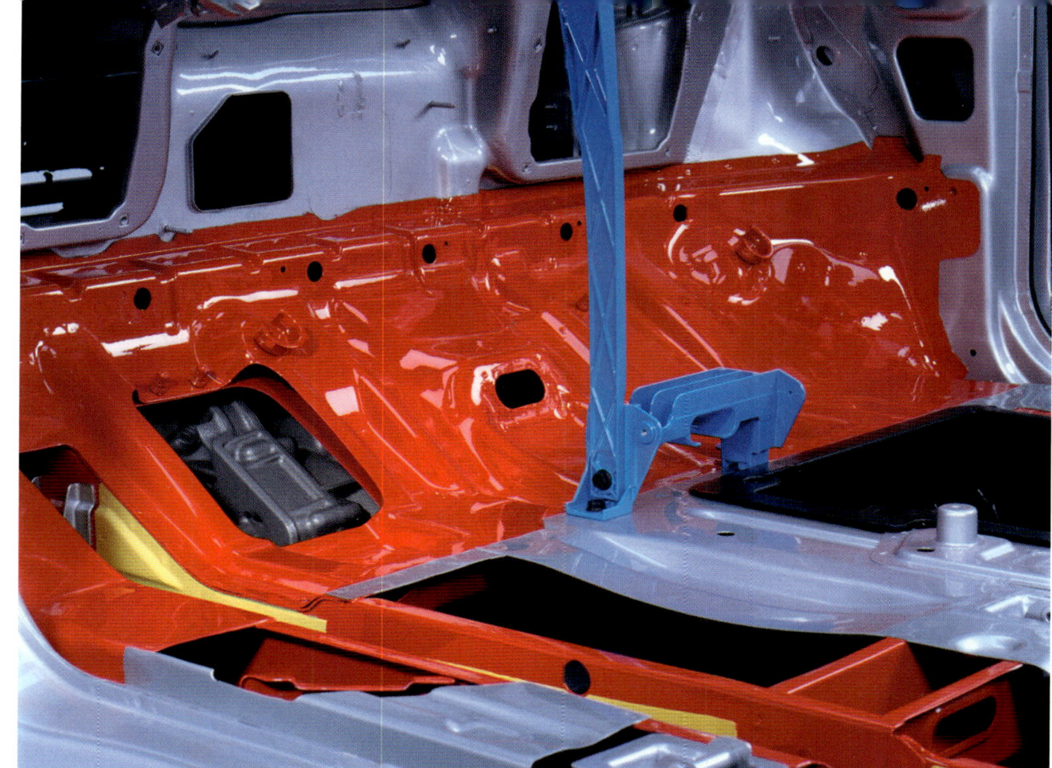

The double-skin floor would deflect all engineering down to the road in the case of a frontal impact, protecting the car's occupants.

BELOW: **Multi-positioning of seats made the A168 very versatile.**

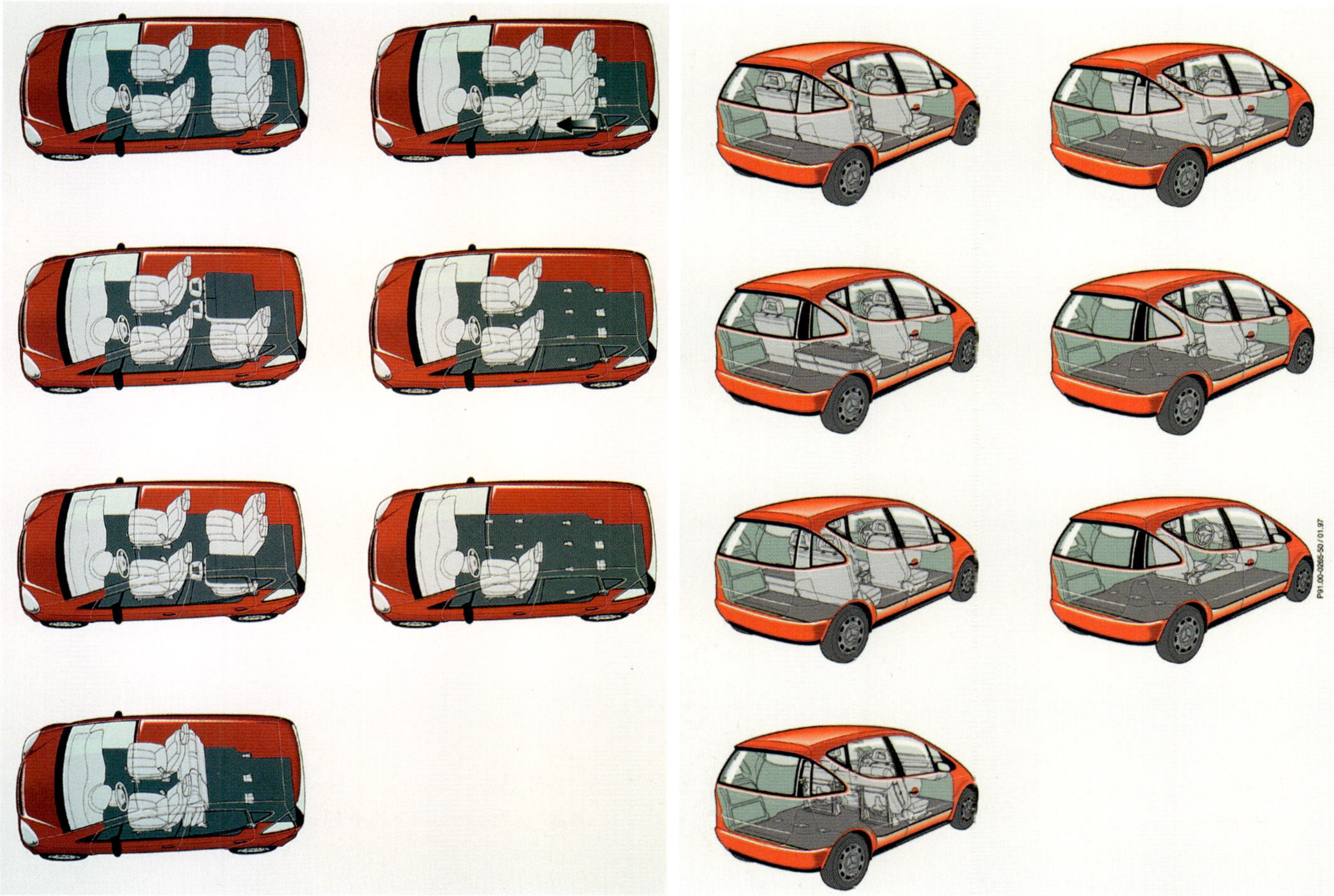

when, on 19 April 1996, the relevant contracts were signed in Brasilia: from the end of 1998, around 1,500 employees in Juiz de Fora, situated between Rio de Janeiro and Belo Horizonte, were to begin producing 70,000 units a year for the South American market.

On 20 May 1996, the A Class again took centre stage when the advertising and communication campaign was launched in Germany and six other European countries via television commercials, adverts in printed media and the internet. There was evidence to show that buyers start researching cars 12 to 18 months prior to purchase, so an early start was vital. Because Mercedes Benz had created the A Class as a totally new vehicle category and potential customers had no predecessor model to refer to, it was all the more important to familiarize interested parties with the future product as early as possible.

Shortly before this, the W168, as the A Class was known internally, had passed various crash tests at the Sindelfingen development centre, demonstrating that even a compact vehicle with short crumple zones could achieve the high safety standards of Mercedes Benz. This was primarily due to the new sandwich-design body, which was divided into two horizontal planes, one above the other. The passenger compartment took up the upper area, while the drive assemblies were positioned at an angle in front of and below the intermediate floor. In a frontal collision, the drive unit would slide away beneath the passenger cell, presenting no risk of injury to the occupants. The A Class not only complied with future EU directives on frontal collisions, but also met the stringent safety requirements set by the European Union and the USA with regard to lateral collisions.

The first official information and photos of the final series-produced version of the vehicle were released to the press at the beginning of December 1996, and the world premiere of the A Class followed three months later at the Geneva Motor Show. Just two months after the presentation of the CLK in Detroit, this event marked a further milestone in the Mercedes Benz strategic product initiative.

CLK W208

When it comes to headlights it is better to set trends than to follow them....I believe that the 'eyes' of the E-Class were indeed revolutionary but they also preserved the identity of the Mercedes brand.

The unveiling of the new coupé study at the 1993 Geneva Motor Show heralded a new era of stylistic freedom for Mercedes designers. It was thought that the relaxing of the original strict guidelines set down by Bruno Sacco would unleash greater innovative power. At the same time, the study announced to the world something never seen before on a Mercedes car: the twin-headlamp face of the future E-Class. It also laid the foundation for the replacement of the coupé to a more generic style called the CLK.

In 1997 the CLK coupé was presented in Geneva. For some reviewers, this model reached the zenith of perfection, the restyled classicism of the E-Class followed by the aggressive character of the SLK, a roadster conceived for the new generations.

The Mercedes-Benz CLK had its world premiere at the North American International Auto Show in Detroit in January 1997. Its big brother, the 140 series coupé, had also been introduced there five years earlier. The European premiere took place one month later at the Amsterdam International Motor Show AutoRAI, and shortly thereafter the new coupé series was displayed at the Geneva Motor Show. It was an important event in the CLK's history.

Mercedes-Benz had provoked some excitement there in March 1993 with a coupé study that vowed to set new standards in close-to-series design. For the first time a completely new interpretation of the Mercedes' bold 'face' had been shown. It was characterized by two pairs of elliptic headlights and more strongly moulded wings, as well as a slender radiator grille. The characteristic 'four-eyes' theme influenced the design of the 210 series E-Class and of the CLK coupés to a significant extent, and this was further encouraged by the extremely positive reactions of the visiting public at and after the Geneva Motor Show. The stylistic design of the CLK editions found its inspiration in the coupé study that was shown in 1993.

At first, the CLK coupé had been developed at Daimler-Benz as an entirely independent model family, a fact that was expressed in the series designation C208. Technically, the CLK was based in many respects on the C-Class saloons, particularly in the borrowing of their floor assembly and units. The individuality of the CLK, however, was clearly visible in numerous deviations from the detail accomplishment and last but not least in the fundamentally different body design.

220 S-CLASS

In 1998 the time was ripe for a new S-Class, a stunning flagship, embodying state-of-the-art design and technology. The Mercedes-Benz S-Class 220 series was officially introduced at the Paris Motor Show at the end of September 1998 and sales began at European dealerships and distributors on 24 October.

With its elegant and dynamic look and numerous innovations, the new S-Class was a worthy successor to the 140 series. Just like its predecessor, it was a trendsetter in automotive technology. Over thirty technological innovations with a total of 340 patents were incorporated in the saloon, including many that were being introduced to the world for the first time. A number of those innovations were standard in the S-Class.

When the specifications book for the replacement of the 140 came out in 1993, it had been on the market for two years and the new development targets not only appeared highly demanding but also somewhat self-contradictory but we had 'been there' before.

The W220 S-Class was sleeker and more slender than any previous Sonderklasse car.

W220 returned to a blending of headlights, moving away from the 'four eyes'.

The interior was **Sonderklasse**.

The rear of the **W220** offered ample legroom for even the tallest of executives.

The **M-Class W163** combined off-road agility with on-road class.

W163 M-Class was a multi-purpose vehicle.

Those development targets included improved performance, along with reduced fuel consumption; increased safety and a comprehensive range of equipment, coupled with a reduction in weight; and more room, but with reduced exterior dimensions and a new, slimmer design. The 220 series S-Class demonstrated that Daimler-Benz engineers had succeeded in overcoming these apparent contradictions, whilst making lasting improvements to a model series that was already acknowledged to be of a very high standard.

An elegant, dynamic appearance and a large number of technical innovations gave the new S-Class the necessary quality to continue and further expand on the global success enjoyed by its predecessor model. In its eight-year run, the 220 S-Class sold 186,733 units.

M-CLASS

The development of M-Class design was based on an accurate analysis of the stylistic features of the models of this segment, revealing that all-terrain vehicles were originally conceived for military or commercial use. The new trend was clearly to use these vehicles as private cars as well. For the M-Class this meant a combination of the character of an elegant station wagon and the sporty qualities of an off-roader.

Aimed principally at the US market, development of the M-Class officially began in 1993. Although attributed to Bruno Sacco, its design was jointly developed between the Advanced Design Studio, located in Irvine, CA, and headed by Gerhard Steinle, and the German studio in Sindelfingen, headed by Peter Pfeiffer.

The exterior design was approved in late 1994 and patented in January 1995. Before its official launch in 1997, a concept car named AAV (All-Activity Vehicle) was unveiled at the Detroit Motor Show in 1996 as a drill. This concept was fully developed in the Californian studio with Gerhard Steinle at the helm, and the design team included Benjamin Dimson, Paul Terry, Melonee Ranzinger, Richard Plavetich, Greg Greeson and Peter Arcadipane, who was the lead exterior designer. The concept was much praised by the press and Gerhard Steinle received the IDEA Gold Award.

CHAPTER SIX

SACCO'S LEGACY

On a bright sunny day at the end of June 1999, Bruno Sacco retired from Daimler-Benz. He was honoured on that occasion by Juergen Schrempp, president of the company:

Bruno Sacco's cars make up an entirely separate period in our legendary history of making motor vehicles.…Without your contribution as artist, carmaker and manager, Mercedes-Benz would certainly not be this rich in meaning nor as unique in the market place.

NEW DESIGN BUILDING

The Mercedes-Benz Design Centre at Sindelfingen, completed in 1998, was commissioned by Bruno Sacco, head of the company's style centre at the time. Mercedes-Benz entrusted Italian architect Renzo Piano with the task of designing the building.

A new design centre was long overdue. 'It was a necessity,' Bruno Sacco explained. 'Design studios and their respective modelling shops were scattered over separate buildings and far distances seriously hindered efficient communication. My superiors were generous and far-sighted to let me have Renzo Piano.' The two Italians – the chief designer and the great architect – immediately found a perfect mutual understanding. Bruno Sacco played a particularly active role in the design of the interior of the new building. 'The interior meets the need to allow for a logical workflow: the design staff, on top; the technical staff who make it possible to put it into practice, in the middle; the building of the models, the bottom.'

The client required the creation of an ideal environment to foster the collaborative creative process that enabled the design of the various Mercedes-Benz ranges. At the same time, certain spaces were reserved exclusively for designers, whose work had to be protected from prying eyes. The shape of the assigned site inspired the fan configuration, so that the building was distinguished by the orthogonal grid of the other new buildings. Piano's first sketches proposed a building with orthogonal organization, in homage to both the outline and the rectilinear nature of the most important elements of the interior: the portals and the parallel benches of lights under which the models would be sculpted in full size. It was Sacco who suggested a freer, 'less Bauhaus' form. The radial plan and the disciplined curves of the roofs of the finished building are adapted to the context in the same way as the original proposal, but are more celebratory.

The building resembles an open hand, in which each element has a different function: design, CAD drafting, model-making and prototyping. There is also a special area where a controllable, semi-transparent light wing ceiling allows the presentation of new vehicles under simulated daylight conditions. In addition, the hand-shaped configuration responds perfectly to the internal functions. The seven fingers are progressively longer, starting from the one to the south. The two naves to the north rise beyond a second building dedicated to administration, to define the triangular square from which the building is entered. The roofs on the aisles of the studios are curved in both directions. The faces of the inside walls are simply plastered and painted white, while on the outside they are covered with narrow Alucobond panels, a composite material in sheets whose external aluminium surface is kept perfectly smooth by a polyethylene backing sheet. The sloped windows, placed high for safety reasons, not only follow the internal work levels that are decreasing in height, but also allow more light to come in as the spans become wider. The enormous coverage with variable section – light, curved, in tension – seems to twist and float freely on the walls.

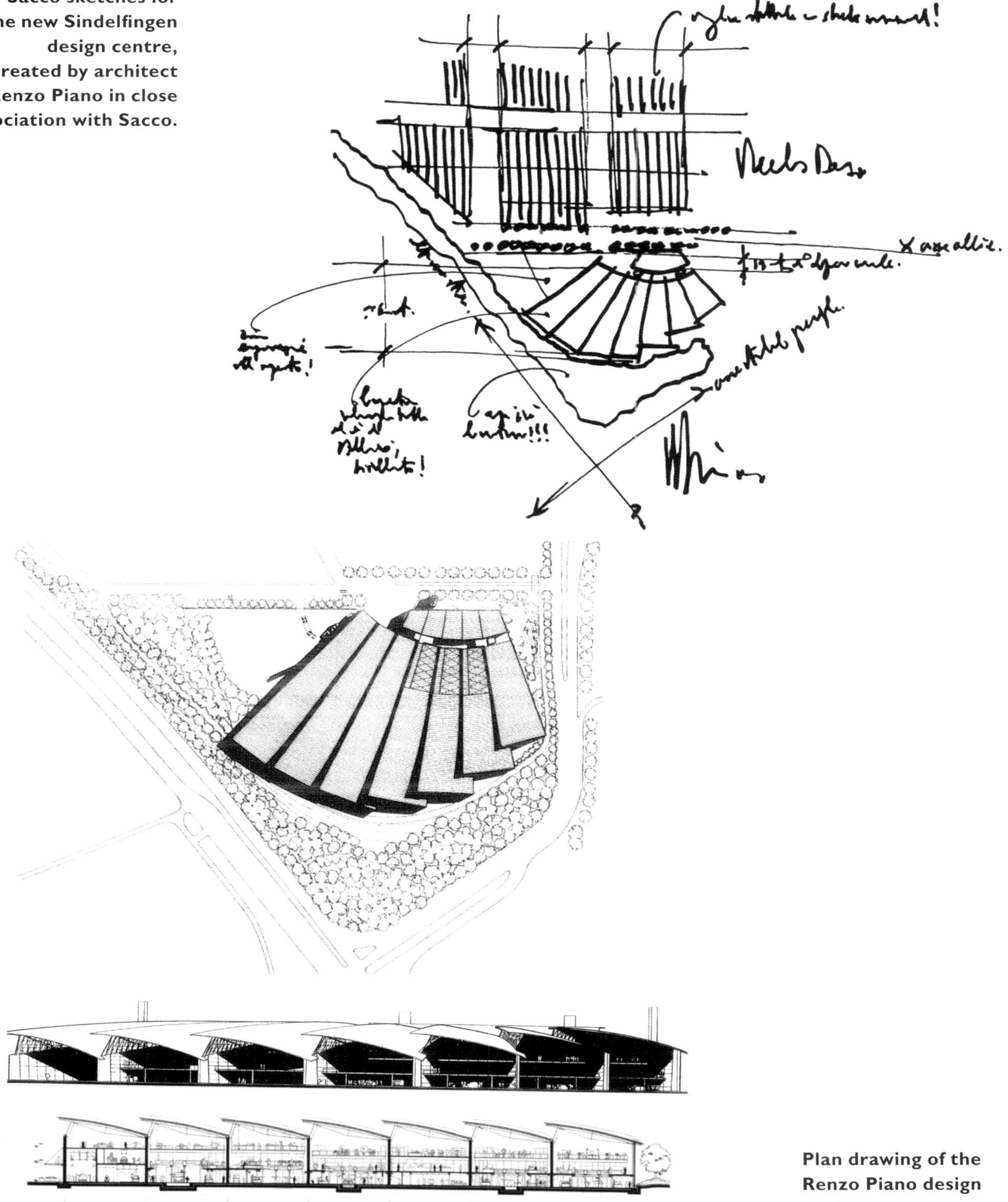

Early Sacco sketches for the new Sindelfingen design centre, created by architect Renzo Piano in close association with Sacco.

Plan drawing of the Renzo Piano design centre.

The free design area at Sindelfingen.

BELOW: **Exterior view.**

Italian architect Renzo Piano.

The Design Centre coordinates and directs the activities of the company's Advanced Design Studios in Carlsbad, Tokyo, Como, and develops the design of the group's production models. The 30,000-square-metre facility employs more than 400 people from over twenty countries.

THE BRUNO SACCO DESIGN LEGACY

For Mercedes-Benz the subject of brand identity has always been at the core of every automobile they have made since 1926. However, what was a Mercedes? What is a Mercedes? They had to be the main questions that every designer would have to ask themselves every day they turned up for work, to ensure that every new vehicle is provided with a distinctive identity and that its premium-brand provenance is immediately apparent.

'A Mercedes-Benz will always be recognisable as a Mercedes-Benz', said Bruno Sacco on many occasions. Although these questions are easy to answer in a shallow way, as today everyone knows what a Mercedes looks like, there is another even more relevant question: what will be a Mercedes? Long-term strategies and theoretical continuity are absolutely necessary in order to develop and maintain such a successful brand image.

Bruno Sacco's legacy of vertical affinity and horizontal homogeneity pointed the way to the future, to ensure their essential lines did not depart from their root origins which in turn provided the brand with a distinctive identity and by doing so the premium-brand provenance was always immediately apparent. At the same time, for the brand to stand apart from its competitors it meant that fashion fads are never an option for the Mercedes designers, they lack the long-term effect that is integral to Mercedes-Benz. He ensured that the high market value that Mercedes passenger cars retain even after many years is attributable not least of all to the fact that an earlier Mercedes-Benz does not look old. Even when follow-up models are premiered their predecessors do not pale in comparison, but remain desirable propositions, above all because their design is made to last.

Design lines alone are not the only consideration: they may provide an immediate visual perspective but Bruno Sacco knew naturally that it wasn't enough to have a beautiful car. Design had to also appeal to the emotions, however, which would, in turn, instil an emotional enthusiasm for the automobile and making a model a true object of desire. 'Love at first sight' may have been a common slogan for many automobile manufacturers, but didn't last. Design must not only arouse such immediate positive emotions, but also sustain them over many years; it needed to create a psychological tie that evolved into recognition through identification. Beyond developing attractive and functional individual products, design thus also needs to create brand adoration.

What Bruno Sacco did was to devote meticulous care to ensuring that certain stylistic features always retain their essential design in the course of their ongoing development. In connection to this he referred to what he called the brand's 'gene pool', on which they draw to maintain and facelift the brand. A good example of this is the trademark Mercedes radiator grille, as mentioned previously; it remained a feature that has characterised and distinguished every Mercedes automobile for over 100 years. Even though its design has undergone continuous development over this time the designers still managed to reinterpret both the basic proportions and the details of this identifying feature in order to create a fresh and modern appearance. Even when the elongated Sports Light version was introduced in the 1950s, the principle's integrity held true. Being adopted directly from motor racing in the 1950s, it was immediately connected as a symbol for the Mercedes sports cars.

Such a detailed approach keeps the design and brand image alive, innovative and dynamic while retaining their own distinctive character. Mercedes-Benz has manage to successfully pursue this strategy for decades, and by doing so establishing itself in new market segments, winning over new customers to the brand and also performing an important trend-setting role.

Trends and reality

Bruno Sacco detested 'fashionable twiddles', saying they immediately dated a style when another trend replaced it or made it obsolete. However, he still recognised that identifying and shaping trends was a key task for any car designers. Even though they had to live in the present and recognize what was desirable, their real business is the future. This not only required a very finely tuned understanding of changes in customers' habits, new attitudes to daily life and aesthetic or colour trends domestically, but other cultures also provide a source of inspiration. It has always been of crucial importance for Mercedes-Benz to be modern without slavishly following the latest fashions and looking into the future and tracking down new trends in this way are not enough on their own.

Daimler AG set up 'Advanced Design Studios' throughout the world; these served as seismographs, recording and analysing stylistic trends. The challenge was to consider possible future developments, thereby thinking beyond the immediate reality shaped by trends and fashions, asking what trends are actually suitable as a source of inspiration for a brand such as Mercedes-Benz. This involved intuitively picking up on developments that might be suitable for incorporation into timeless design, and acquiring an instinct for important, lasting trends in art, culture, and society.

Passion and rationality

'Motoring today is no longer simply a matter of driving from A to B in safety and comfort. I endeavoured to make every journey, an experience for the senses in its own right. It wasn't just about 'where you sat in the car' it was how it made you feel, what you could see and reach out and touch, even the air on your face…

Its all about the sense of pride you felt looking out from your cocoon and seeing others looking in at you'

This focus on peoples feeling is perhaps the most important and interesting aspect defining automobile designers' work. Bruno Sacco saw very early in his careers that discerning customers wanted more from their automotive experience, the feel of achieving the 'the finer things in life' and being willing to be proud, yet humble, at their achievement. This sensual perception of a product played a prominent role during his tenure.

Maintaining the appeal of attractive appointments over many years and many models of automobile is an extremely important part of design. Customers have definitely become more demanding and sensitive in this respect in recent years. The interior of a car is no longer just seen as a 'cabin' but as a 'personal space'. It has become an environment in which people spend a great deal of time and ensuring it is always a pleasant environment has becoming increasingly important. In addition to a diverse range of trims and appointments from which they can pick and choose according to their own individual tastes and personalities, they also attach special importance to high-quality materials and excellent workmanship. These communicate values such as aesthetics, comfort and quality in a directly perceptible manner in the context of the overall visual impression.

The aim of the interior design in Mercedes-Benz automobiles can be summed up in a few words: on boarding the vehicle and closing the doors, users should feel at home immediately. Surrounded by attractive forms, their eyes take in valuable, handcrafted fine wood trims as they enjoy the feel of soft leather seat surfaces and the look of pleasant, warm colours. This is the world of Mercedes-Benz.

(Bruno Sacco)

AWARDS

During the years he worked at Daimler-Benz, Bruno Sacco received numerous personal awards:

1981: Honorary member of the Academia Mexicana de Diseño

1991: Received the title Grande Ufficiale dell'Ordine al Merito della Repubblica Italiana

1993: Winner of the Cover Award, Auto & Design, Turin

1993: Awarded the Premio Mexico 1994, Patronato Nacional de las Asociaciones de Diseño AC, Mexico

1994: Winner of the Apulia Award for Professional Achievement

1996: Voted Best Designer by *Car* magazine

1996: Voted Designers' Designer by *Car* magazine

1997: Winner of the Lifetime Design Achievement Award, Detroit

1997: Presented with the Raymond Loewy Designer Award by the Lucky Strike brand

2002: Honorary doctorate from the Udine University, Italy

2006: Inducted into the Automotive Hall of Fame, Dearborn

2007: Inducted into the European Automotive Hall of Fame, Geneva

Bruno Sacco was inducted into the Automotive Hall of Fame (Dearborn, Michigan) on 3 October 2006.

BATHROOM PRODUCTS

Following his retirement in 1999, Bruno Sacco rejected numerous offers from various car manufacturers. He vowed never to design automobiles again and in 2001 the Hansa bathroom company secured him as a design consultant. This led to a collaboration with Reinhard Zetsche and to the design successes of high-end bathroom appliances in the HANSA EDITION, HANSA MURANO, HANSA CANYON and HANSA LATRAVA Series.

The functional design is combined with an intense emotionality of the senses. All of them refer to the philosophy inspired by HANSA, 'Living the water', in its purest form. Collections are based on the concept of exclusivity and aimed at a target sensitive to the themes of architecture and design.

Bruno Sacco collaborated with Reinhard Zetsche on the HANSA MURANO bathroom appliance.

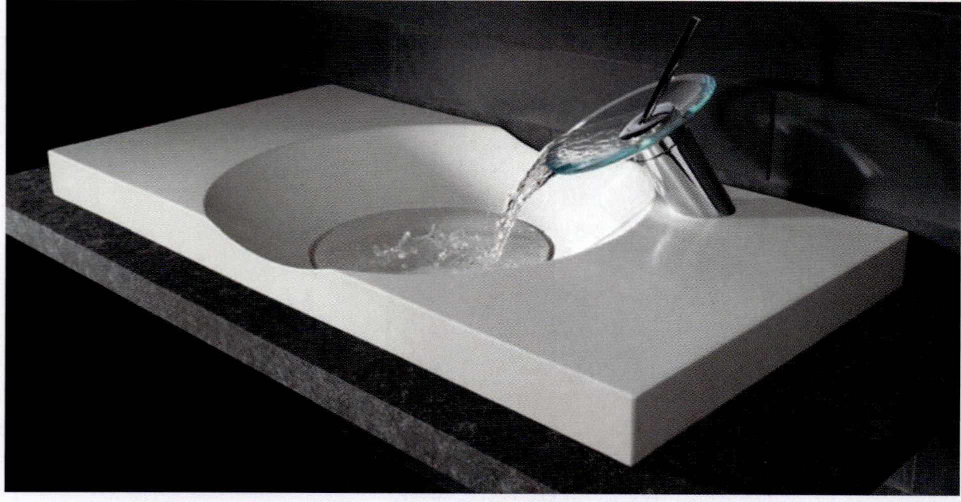

Taking its cue from classical fountains, the HANSA MURANO has a stylish flow pattern that gently pours over an elegant glass surface.

The **HANSA LATRAVA** is like a formal sculpture.

The water jet is given a shape in direct continuation with the structure of the tap.

The **HANSA EDITION** bathroom appliance, designed by Bruno Sacco.

Visions and emotions

Bruno Sacco played an enormous part in the development of Experimental research, show cars, and concept vehicles, none of which should be taken lightly. He convinced the board at Daimler-Benz on many occasions that carrying out such car studies was necessary for exploring future styles, and to offer designers a means of developing and realising new design idioms. Every individual test model was developed to lend concrete form to automotive visions, to test new vehicle concepts or technologies, to intensify the dialogue with customers and to analyse the public's reaction to such automotive ideas.

Whether it is a research vehicle or standard production vehicle, an automobile is always perceived on a sensual level.

It has become the task of every designer to not only arouse these emotions but to keep them alive. Its emotional impact must be all consuming. Long before any technical data, innovation or mechanical appointments become apparent, desires are aroused by a car's appearance alone. That is the job of the designer. Only after this, the object of their work becomes the job to reconcile technology and design so as to develop automobiles that boast both technical and emotional intelligence.

Bruno Sacco summed it up when he said that a successful design is one in which no one sees the designer but an object of desire. The automotive designer knows that their design was a success when customers buy their cars without rationale or being overly analytical, but on listening to their hearts and minds in equal portion.

INDEX